John 1-3

MATT CHANDLER

Lifeway Press®
Nashville, Tennessee

Editorial Team

Susan Hill
Writer

Jennifer Siao
Production Editor

Reid Patton
Content Editor

Jon Rodda
Art Director

Joel Polk
Editorial Team Leader

Brian Daniel
Manager, Short-Term Discipleship

Brandon Hiltibidal
Director, Discipleship & Groups Ministry

Ben Mandrell
President, Lifeway Christian Resources

Published by Lifeway Press® • © 2021 The Village Church

ISBN 978-1-0877-4172-7 • Item 005831473

Dewey decimal classification: 226.5
Subject headings: BIBLE. N.T. JOHN 1-3 / JESUS CHRIST / CHRISTIAN LIFE

Unless otherwise noted, Scripture quotations are taken from the ESV® Bible (The Holy Bible, English Standard Version®), copyright © 2001 by Crossway, a publishing ministry of Good News Publishers. Used by permission. All rights reserved.

Scripture quotations marked (MSG) are taken from THE MESSAGE. Copyright © by Eugene H. Peterson 1993, 1994, 1995, 1996, 2000, 2001, 2002. Used by permission of NavPress. All rights reserved. Represented by Tyndale House Publishers, Inc.

To order additional copies of this resource, write to Lifeway Resources Customer Service; One Lifeway Plaza; Nashville, TN 37234; fax 615-251-5933; phone toll free 800-458-2772; order online at Lifeway.com; or email orderentry@lifeway.com.

Printed in the United States of America

Adult Ministry Publishing • Lifeway Resources
One Lifeway Plaza • Nashville, TN 37234

Contents

ABOUT THE AUTHOR

MATT CHANDLER serves as the lead pastor of teaching at The Village Church in the Dallas/Fort Worth metroplex. He came to The Village in December 2002 and describes his tenure as a replanting effort to change the theological and philosophical culture of the congregation.

Alongside his current role as lead pastor, Matt is involved in church-planting efforts both locally and internationally through The Village, as well as in various strategic partnerships. Prior to accepting the pastorate at The Village, Matt had a vibrant itinerant ministry for more than ten years that gave him the opportunity to speak to thousands of people in America and abroad about the glory of God and the beauty of Jesus.

Matt is the author of *Take Heart; To Live Is Christ, to Die Is Gain; Mingling of Souls; The Explicit Gospel* Bible study, *The Apostles' Creed* Bible study, and the *James* Bible study. He's also a coauthor of *Creature of the Word*.

Other than knowing Jesus, Matt's greatest joy is being married to Lauren and being the dad to their three children: Audrey, Reid, and Norah.

ABOUT THE GOSPEL OF JOHN

The Gospel of John is different from the Synoptic Gospels—Matthew, Mark, and Luke—in that more than ninety percent of its material is unique. John's Gospel does not focus on the miracles, parables, and public speeches that are so prominent in the other accounts. Instead, the Gospel of John emphasizes the identity of Jesus as the Son of God and how we, as believers, should respond to his teachings.

Of all the Gospels and any of the New Testament books, the Gospel of John most clearly teaches the deity and preexistence of Christ (1:1–2, 18; 8:58; 17:5, 24; 20:28). John portrays Jesus as the eternal Word of God who became flesh to redeem His people from their sins.

HOW TO USE THIS STUDY

John 1-3: The Word Became Flesh provides a guided process for individuals and small groups to walk through the Gospel of John. This Bible study book includes twelve weeks of content, each divided into three major sections: "Group Study," "Family Discipleship," and "Personal Study." A leader guide is also provided to prepare those who are leading groups through this journey.

GROUP STUDY

Regardless of the day of the week your group meets, each week of content begins with a group session. This group session is designed to last ninety minutes, with approximately forty-five minutes dedicated to video teaching and another forty-five minutes to group discussion. Meeting even longer than ninety minutes will allow more time for participants to interact with one another.

Each group study uses the following format to facilitate simple yet meaningful interaction among group members, with God's Word, and with the video teaching.

START

This section includes questions to get the conversation started, a review of the previous week's study to reinforce the content, and an introduction to the new content for the current week.

WATCH

This section includes key points from the video teaching, along with space for taking notes as participants watch the video.

DISCUSS

This section includes discussion questions that guide the group to respond to the video teaching and to relevant Bible passages. A second page has been provided to take notes and write down prayer requests.

FAMILY DISCIPLESHIP

John 1-3: The Word Became Flesh presents a great opportunity for families to consider the truths of John's Gospel together. The weekly "Family Discipleship" section provides discussion and activities that encourage families to engage with this material on a deeper level.

This section will guide your family to consider the truths of the gospel by utilizing the following framework: "Time," "Moments," and "Milestones." Use this framework for family discipleship in your home and on the go. Additionally, you'll read Scripture together and restate the main point of the week's group session.

PERSONAL STUDY

Two personal studies are provided each week to take individuals deeper into Scripture and to supplement the content introduced in the group study. With biblical teaching and interactive questions, these sections challenge individuals to grow in their understanding of God's Word and to make practical application to their lives.

LEADER GUIDE

On pages 152-161 at the back of this book, you'll find a leader guide that will help you prepare each week. Use this guide to gain a broad understanding of the content for each week and to learn ways you can engage with members at different levels of life-changing discussion.

Through the Word

GROUP STUDY

Start
Welcome everyone to session 1.

Ask participants to introduce themselves with quick answers to the following question:

What's one phrase, nickname, or fact that summarizes who you are?

Today we begin our study of the Gospel of John. John's Gospel differs from Matthew, Mark, and Luke (known as the Synoptic Gospels) in a variety of ways, The other three Gospels share similar language, structure, and stories. John approaches Jesus' life from a different perspective and includes accounts not found anywhere else in the New Testament. Only John's Gospel includes Jesus' "I Am" statements, the story of the Samaritan woman at the well, Jesus raising Lazarus from the dead, and Jesus' Farewell Discourse (John 14–17).

What are your hopes for studying during these next 12 weeks?

John's Gospel has been described as simple enough for a child to understand and deep enough to drown an elephant. John's Gospel gives us a beautiful portrait of the person and work of Jesus Christ.

To prepare for video session 1, pray that God will help each person understand and apply this truth:

> Jesus is the Christ, the Son of God, and
> you may have life in His name.

Watch

*Use the space below to take notes while
you watch video session 1.*

Video sessions available at lifeway.com/johnbiblestudy

Discuss

*Use the following questions to guide
your discussion of the video.*

1. Pastor Matt said, "Jesus is not a philosopher or some sort of moral teacher; instead, He is the Christ, the very Son of God." How do your non-believing friends think about Jesus? What led them to think about Jesus in this way?

2. John revealed that his reason for writing was so readers would understand that "Jesus is the Son of God and so they could have life in His name" (John 20:31). How is it possible to believe that Jesus is the Son of God but fail to have life in His name?

3. How does John 20:30-31 eliminate the possibility that Jesus was merely a philosopher, moral teacher, or prophet? Why is an accurate understanding of Jesus' identity foundational to our faith?

4. Read John 14:6 and Acts 4:12. How do Luke's words in Acts 4:12 echo John's teaching?

5. John 1:1 describes Jesus as the Word. Pastor Matt taught, "The Word of God is described several times in the Old Testament as one sent forth by God to accomplish the purposes of God and then returns to God." Read Isaiah 55:11. Describe the similarities you see between this passage and the way Pastor Matt described Jesus as the Word.

6. Read 2 Timothy 3:16-17. According to this passage, who is the Author of Scripture? Why is the Word of God valuable to believers? How do the Scriptures help us know Jesus?

7. Share about a time you've been convicted, taught, guided, comforted, or encouraged by the Word of God.

8. What remaining questions or comments do you have about this session's video teaching or discussion? What was challenging, convicting, encouraging, or timely for your current circumstances?

PRAYER REQUESTS

FAMILY DISCIPLESHIP

The Gospel of John teaches us about the person and work of Jesus Christ. The Christian life involves learning how to live out what we believe about Jesus. Each week this "Family Discipleship" section will help parents walk alongside their children and lead them toward Christ by sharing the truths they're learning from the Gospel of John.

"Family Discipleship" will follow a simple, three-part format: time, moments, and milestones. Spend time together as a family in God's Word. Look for moments throughout the day to reinforce the main truth of the week. Celebrate and remember milestones—significant ways God has worked in your lives.

■ **TIME:** Read John 1:1-5. Encourage children to read the Bible if they're able. Take turns reading the verses out loud. Explain that Jesus has always existed and that He is God. Help children understand that Jesus created everything, and since He created everything—including us, Jesus knows what is best for us.

■ **MOMENTS:** Look for opportunities to point out things Jesus has created, especially as it relates to their daily lives. Examples might include the sky, sun, moon, trees, flowers, animals, and all of creation. Emphasize the joy of acknowledging God's creation.

■ **MILESTONES:** Ask children to name their favorite Bible stories and share what they like about them. Talk about what it means for someone to write a biography about another person's life. Explain that John's Gospel tells the story of Jesus' life, and Jesus' story was written by God because the Bible is God's Word. Now your family will spend time each week reading that book and learning about Jesus.

Personal Study 1
THE WORD WAS GOD

If you ever wrote a research paper when you were in school, you know the value of a good thesis statement. A thesis statement declares your purpose for writing and guides the reader's expectations. Generally speaking, thesis statements usually come early in a manuscript, but John reveals his purpose near the end of his Gospel.

Read John 20:30-31. Why did John write his Gospel?

John wrote his Gospel to demonstrate that Jesus is the Son of God and that by believing in Him, we may have life in His name. Understanding this thesis gives us insight as we read John's Gospel. Although his thesis comes late in the book, John begins to address Jesus' identity from the opening verses:

In the beginning was the Word, and the Word was with God, and the Word was God. He was in the beginning with God. All things were made through him, and without him was not any thing made that was made. In him was life, and the life was the light of men. The light shines in the darkness, and the darkness has not overcome it.
JOHN 1:1-5

Spend a few minutes reviewing the passage above. List every fact that John reveals to us about Jesus.

What stands out to you in this passage?

Matthew and Luke begin with a genealogy and birth account, but John takes a different approach. He immediately begins to offer proof for his thesis. In the first sentence, John reveals the thrust of his book, that Jesus is the Christ, the Son of God, and that in Him is life. And this Jesus that John writes about came to earth and put on flesh to live among us.

Spend a moment thinking about the fact that Jesus has always been and will always be, but He put on flesh and dwelt among us. Why is it significant that Jesus came to earth and dwelt among us?

What all did Jesus leave to come to us? Why does this matter?

God Made Visible

John is very concerned that we understand who Jesus is. The primary way we come to know God is through the study of the Scriptures. When we want to know what God is like—His character, attributes, and how He responded in specific situations—we need to take a close look at how He revealed Himself in the Bible.

Read Colossians 1:15-17. How do these words reinforce the themes we find in John 1:1-5?

What does it mean for Jesus to be made in the image of the invisible God?

When we think about what God is like, our knee-jerk reaction, because of our humanity, is to believe God is disappointed, angry, frustrated, and regrets saving us. But Jesus, who is God in the flesh, shows us a very different picture. If we want to understand what God is like, we need to pay special attention to how Jesus acted in the Gospels. How did He treat sinners? The sick? The lost? What made Him angry? What caused Him to weep? How did outsiders respond to Him? If we want to have a thriving relationship with God, we'll have to throw out any preconceived notions about Him that don't align with how He presents Himself in the Scriptures.

Spend a couple of minutes thinking about God. How would you describe Him? What is He like?

What do you believe that God thinks about you?

What informs how you think God sees you? Your past sins or what God says about you in Scripture?

Do you suspect you have ideas about the character of God that can't be confirmed by Scripture? If so, what are they?

It's hard for some of us to wrap our minds around the reality that there is a loving God who wants to have a relationship with us—despite our sinful nature and the ways we've failed Him. But Jesus Christ is proof of that reality. Jesus is fully aware of our sins and shortcomings—it's the reason He took on flesh and came to dwell here on earth—so we could be reconciled to God.

Conclude your study by praying through the following questions.

Am I as close to Jesus as I would like to be? If not, what is holding me back?

Ask God to reveal any errors in your understanding of Him. Pray that as you study His Word, you will learn new things about His character.

Personal Study 2
LIFE AND LIGHT

*In him was life, and the life was the light of men. The light shines
in the darkness, and the darkness has not overcome it.*
JOHN 1:4-5

A close look at John's Gospel reveals two words that appear over and over: "life" and "light." The Bible often uses the opposite of these words to describe this world's fallen nature when it speaks of "death" and "darkness." John speaks of light and life as they relate to salvation: the "light" is revelation which can lead to salvation and "life" is the spiritual life that results from Christ's salvation.

According to John, how is life and light connected to Jesus?

How does the light of Christ shine in dark places today?

Remember, John's purpose in writing is so that we might know that Jesus is the Christ, the Son of God, and that life is found in Him. Why? Because you have been made by Him and for Him. We have an invitation from Jesus to come into the life and light that He offers.

Theologian, Frederick Bruner wrote:

> We long to know who God is and what God thinks and does. In Jesus, his most personal Word, God has 'spoken' to us in the most human way possible, giving us his innermost thoughts and heart, in deeds that are as profound as his words, and the believing human race has experienced deep help ever since.

Bruner believed that "In Jesus, God has given his innermost thoughts and heart." What does Jesus' personality reveal about God?

What does Jesus' coming to earth reveal to us about the heart of God?

Echoes of Genesis

In John's opening statement, he declared that "the Word was in the beginning, was with God, and was God" (v. 1). These words echo all the way back to Genesis 1:

> *In the beginning, God created the heavens and the earth.*
> **GENESIS 1:1**

The life and light we read about in John have been around since before the beginning. Jesus is and always has been one with God. He was with God creating and sustaining the world. These passages form the foundation for the church's confession of the doctrine of the Trinity—the belief that God eternally exists as one essense in three distinct persons.

Slowly re-read Genesis 1:1-3 and John 1:1-5. What similarities do you see? What words and themes appear in both places?

One of the most exciting things about the Bible is how the storyline takes place over thousands of years and is conveyed through various authors. How does seeing the theme of Genesis echoed in John's Gospel help you see the full story of Scripture more clearly?

The Light Shines On

*The light shines in the darkness, and the
darkness has not overcome it.*
JOHN 1:5

In the verse above "shines" is a present and a continuing action. Jesus' light continues to shine just as brightly today as it did when these words were written. At times, the darkness in today's world seems overwhelming but we can rest assured that the light of Christ has not dimmed. But if we want to live in the light of Christ, we must follow Him:

*Jesus spoke to them, saying, "I am the light of the world. Whoever
follows me will not walk in darkness, but will have the light of life."*
JOHN 8:12

What did Jesus promise to those who follow Him?

In what areas of your life do you need Jesus to shine light into darkness?

What is your response to Jesus' invitation to follow Him?

*Close your time in prayer by asking God to shine light in areas
of darkness, confusion, and uncertainty. Give thanks to Christ
because He continues even now shining light in dark places.*

1. (RC Sproul, *John: St. Andrews's Expositional Commentary,* (Reformation Trust Publishing: Sanford, 2009), 3-4).
2. Bruner, Frederick Dale. *The Gospel of John: A Commentary*. Grand Rapids, MI: Eerdmans, 2012.

SESSION 2

God-Given Belief

GROUP STUDY

Start
Welcome everyone to session 2.

How do you form opinions about what you believe? Do you read up on topics, listen to the news, get other people's views, and/or come to conclusions on your own?

Can you recall the moment or season of life when you believed the gospel was true? What led up to it?

The word "believe" repeatedly appears in John's writing and is a central theme in his Gospel. To believe is to receive something. What we believe is important because what we believe is foundational to who we are as human beings. We become children of God through belief. What happens when we believe? The Bible says the Spirit of God indwells us and we are transformed by His presence.

Can you think of an instance when you changed your mind about something? What prompted your change of thinking?

To prepare for video session 2, pray that God will help each person understand and apply this truth:

We become children of God by believing in Jesus' name.

Watch

*Use the space below to take notes while
you watch video session 2.*

Video sessions available at lifeway.com/johnbiblestudy

Discuss

*Use the following questions to guide
your discussion of the video..*

1. Pastor Matt said, "You do not become believers because of your bloodlines."
    What did he mean by that?

2. The word "believe" appears numerous times in John's Gospel. To believe, we
    have to receive the gift of belief. How is the act of believing a gift from God?

3. John 1:7 says John the Baptist came to "bear witness about the light, that all
    might believe through him." What role do we have as modern-day believers
    to bear witness about Jesus?

4. Pastor Matt referred to John the Baptist as a "front-runner" to Jesus—the
    one who came heralding the good news. In what ways was John the Baptist
    unique?

5. Who were the people who were instrumental in telling you about Jesus?
    How did their willingness to tell you about Jesus influence you?

6. When is the last time you shared your faith with a non-believer? Are you
    comfortable doing so? If not, what would it take for you to be willing?

7. One of the most effective ways to tell other people about Jesus is to share
    your testimony and explain how your life is different because of Jesus.
    What details would you include in your testimony? How is your life different
    because of your relationship with Jesus?

8. What remaining questions or comments do you have about this session's
    video teaching or discussion? What was challenging, convicting, encouraging,
    or timely for your current circumstances?

PRAYER REQUESTS

FAMILY DISCIPLESHIP

The Gospel of John shows us that we are dependent upon God to help us believe in the name of Jesus and become His children.

If you need to, reword this week's truth so that your whole family can understand it.

■ **TIME:** Read John 1:6-13. Encourage children to read the Scripture if they're able. Take turns reading the verses out loud. Tell them some of the specifics about John the Baptist—that he lived in the wilderness and wore camel haired clothing and ate locusts and wild honey (Matt. 3:4). Include the details that he was a prophet and his job was to tell people about Jesus' coming.

■ **MOMENTS:** During commute times give children opportunities to share what they know and believe about Jesus. Encourage them to ask questions about things they don't understand. Ask them to identify people in their lives who teach people about Jesus like John the Baptist did. Examples might include parents, grandparents, Sunday-school teachers, and extended family members.

■ **MILESTONES:** Encourage your children to identify significant events that have played a role in growing their faith. Explain to them that these milestones are all part of their history with God. Mark significant dates by acknowledging and celebrating.

A MAN SENT FROM GOD

*There was a man sent from God, whose name was
John. He came as a witness, to bear witness about the
light, that all might believe through him. He was not the
light, but came to bear witness about the light.*

JOHN 1:6-8

John the Baptist is one of the most well-known personalities in Scripture. By any standards, his life was anything but ordinary. He was a prophet with a unique mission. His birth was announced by angelic proclamation and divine intervention (Luke 1:57-80), and his early years were lived in solitude in the wilderness (Luke 1:80). The focal point of his ministry was, "Repent, for the kingdom of heaven is at hand" (Matt. 3:2).

Glance back at John 1:6-8. What role did John come to fill? What was the purpose of his calling?

Notice the text says, "He was not the light, but came to bear witness about the light." What does it mean to "bear witness?"

Not many of God's people were called to be prophets, but we are all called to tell others about Jesus. With that in mind, what can we learn from John the Baptist?

John the Baptist wasn't out to make a name for himself. John knew he was subordinate to Jesus. He repeatedly denied that he was the Christ and emphasized he was not the light but merely a witness to the light (1:8). John's role and our role in the kingdom are crucial. God can use any means He chooses to draw people to Himself, but He often uses flesh and blood human beings to draw new believers to the kingdom of God.

Faith Comes From Hearing

Read Romans 10:9-17.

In your own words, describe the correlation between hearing the Word and believing.

Glance back at verses 14-15. How should these verses inform our views about missions and evangelism?

To believe is to receive something. How does hearing God's Word allow us to receive and believe (v. 17)?

The gospel of Jesus Christ must be communicated for people to receive it. Certainly, God calls and equips preachers, evangelists, pastors, and teachers to communicate His Word (Eph. 4:11). But even those who aren't called to full-time vocational ministry are called to share the gospel. When we encounter Jesus and experience His presence in our lives, the most natural response is to tell others. In Scripture, the most common reaction for people who have encountered Jesus is for them to share their experience.

Read through the following passages and write down how each person responded after they encountered Jesus.

John 4:1-29. How did the woman respond in verse 29?

Mark 5:1-20. Pay special attention to verses 19-20. How did the man respond to Jesus' command in verse 19?

Acts 4:1-20. In verse 20, what did Peter and John say to the authorities?

What do these accounts teach us about the value of hearing and responding to the gospel?

As believers, it's our privilege to tell other people about Jesus. We don't have to have the knowledge of our pastor or the eloquent speech of a theologian. The most effective way to communicate our faith is to share what Jesus has done for us and tell how our lives are better because He is our Lord.

Why should you consider it a privilege to tell what Jesus has done for you? What obstacles prevent you from sharing your faith?

Close your time of study by giving thanks to God for the gift of believing. Ask Him to provide you with opportunities to share your faith. Give thanks for the people who invested in your life by sharing the gospel with you.

Personal Study 2
CHILDREN OF GOD

But to all who did receive him, who believed in his name, he gave the right to become children of God.
JOHN 1:12

Evangelism defined John the Baptist's ministry. He told people about Jesus so they would have the opportunity to believe—and in believing—God would give them the right to become children of God. All people begin in darkness, because our sins have separated us from God (Rom. 3:23). But the Bible tells us, a light shines and has come and illuminated the darkness (John 1:5). When the light of Christ shines light in the darkness—and we believe—we become children of God.

Why is it incorrect to say all people are children of God?

What's at stake for those who are not children of God?

Those who reject the light (Jesus) are not children of God. Yes, God created everyone, and therefore all human beings are made in His image (Gen. 1:27), but not everyone knows God as Father The only path to the Father is through the Son. Jesus said, "I am the way, and the truth, and the life. No one comes to the Father except through me" (John 14:6)

You've probably heard the saying, "There are many paths to God." How does John's Gospel demonstrate this isn't true?

Skeptics and non-believers have been known to say that Jesus being the only path to God is rigid or unfair. How would you respond to that?

Son or Slave?

Jesus answered them, "Truly, truly, I say to you, everyone who practices sin is a slave to sin. The slave does not remain in the house forever; the son remains forever. So if the Son sets you free, you will be free indeed."
JOHN 8:34-36

The passage above teaches that if we aren't children of God, we will be slaves to sin. Those are the only two possibilities for all of humankind. Our sin is what separated us from God, and without God's intervention, we will remain in bondage to sin. A slave has no permanent standing in God's house—only a child of God does. So when it comes to what we believe about Jesus—what's at stake is our standing before God—and ultimately eternal life.

How should our belief in Jesus entirely define our lives?

Glance back at John 8:36 above. Apart from Jesus, we are all slaves to sin. Practically speaking, what does this look like?

Sin is an unpopular subject in modern-day culture. Why do you think it's difficult for some people to accept the fact that they are sinners?

How does our sin problem keep us from realizing our need for a Savior?

Fellow Heirs With Christ

The Spirit himself bears witness with our spirit that we
are children of God, and if children, then heirs—heirs of
God and fellow heirs with Christ, provided we suffer with
him in order that we may also be glorified with him.
ROMANS 8:16-17

According to the passage above, what role does the Holy Spirit play in assuring believers that they are indeed children of God?

What does it mean to be a coheir with Christ?

Are you confident you are a child of God? Why or why not?

If you are a child of God, you are an heir of all that God owns. Everything in this world and in the life to come belongs to God. As a child of God, you are no longer a slave to sin. That doesn't mean you won't struggle with sin, but it means that God gives you the power to overcome sin, and because of Jesus' finished work on the cross, you are forgiven of your sins.

See what kind of love the Father has given to us, that we
should be called children of God; and so we are. The reason
why the world does not know us is that it did not know him.
1 JOHN 3:1

Close your time today giving thanks to God that through Jesus He has
provided a way to become a child of God, who is set free from your sins,
a coheir with Christ, and can look forward to spending eternity with Him.

Grace Upon Grace

GROUP STUDY

Start
Welcome everyone to session 3.

Think about the food and supplies you keep stocked in your home. What types of things are you most careful not to run out of?

Can you think of something you'd like to use but you are saving for a "rainy day?"

After the Great Depression, it was common for people to stockpile non-perishable food in their homes. After experiencing a long period of lack, they wanted to be prepared if hard times struck again. For obvious reasons, they had developed a mentality of scarcity that continued even after the Great Depression ended. Without meaning to, some of us view God with a scarcity mentality—we suspect He reigns on the throne with clenched fists. But by believing this, we misunderstand His character and carry a burden He doesn't want us to carry.

Do you tend to think of God as tight-fisted or open-handed? Explain.

To prepare for video session 3, pray that God will help each person understand and apply this truth:

> Those who believe in the finished work of Jesus experience a well of abundant grace that never runs dry.

Watch

Use the space below to take notes
while you watch video session 3.

Video sessions available at lifeway.com/johnbiblestudy

Discuss

*Use the following questions to guide
your discussion of the video.*

1. What is the difference between a scarcity mentality and an abundance mentality?

2. How might we have a scarcity mentality with God? How does such a mentality warp our view of God and His grace?

3. How does confidence in God's grace lighten our burdens and free us from the feeling of scarcity?

4. Where might our fears about scarcity originate? Have you ever experienced a time when you worried yourself sick over the fear that God wouldn't come through? Share your experience.

5. Pastor Matt said, "What God calls us to, then, He provides for, but the primary provision God brings to us is not wealth, health, and power; it's grace." What did he mean by that statement?

6. How do people get God's provision confused with the "wealth and health" prosperity gospel? Why is the teaching that the gospel will give us material blessing contrary to Scripture?

7. Even though the prosperity gospel isn't true, the Scriptures do teach that God is faithful to provide for our needs. Pastor Matt said, "What He calls you to, He will provide for." Have you experienced this to be true? If so, explain.

8. What does it mean to abound? How does this correlate with the idea of an abundance mentality rather than a scarcity mentality?

PRAYER REQUESTS

FAMILY DISCIPLESHIP

Those who believe in the finished work
of Jesus experience a well of abundant
grace that never runs dry.

**If you need to, reword this week's truth so that your whole
family can understand it.**

■ **TIME:** Read John 1:14-18. Encourage children to read the Scripture
if they're able. Take turns reading the verses out loud. Bring special
attention to the phrase, "the Word became flesh and dwelt among us"
(John 1:14). Explain that the Word made flesh refers to Jesus. Emphasize
that the Scripture says Jesus is full of grace and truth. Explain how these
verses teach us this week's truth.

■ **MOMENTS:** When a child doesn't do what he or she is asked, look for
opportunities to explain the concept of grace. Provide examples of how
even when we make mistakes, God continues to love and provide for us.
Explain that we all need grace and we have opportunities to show grace
to other people, including our parents, siblings, and friends.

■ **MILESTONES:** Talk about the ways God has shown you grace in your
own life. Tell your children about key moments when you've needed
grace and provide examples of ways you've shown grace in specific situations. Emphasize that we all need grace and we also need to be people
who extend grace to others.

Personal Study 1
THE WORD BECAME FLESH

And the Word became flesh and dwelt among us, and we have seen his glory, glory as of the only Son from the Father, full of grace and truth.
JOHN 1:14

One of the most powerful phrases in John's Gospel is "the Word became flesh and dwelt among us" (1:14). The phrase at the end of that verse could also be translated "tabernacled among us." In the Book of Exodus, the tabernacle was the place that sat at the middle of the Jewish encampment where the presence and power of God dwelt among the Hebrews. From this point, they could always look up and see a pillar of clouds or fire, and they would know the presence of God was with them. Now John is saying, "The tabernacle is among us. The Word of God has put on flesh, and He is here."

In all other major world religions, people make attempts to get to God. In Christianity, God came to us in flesh and blood as Jesus Christ. How does this make Christianity distinct?

What does Christ's coming teach us about the heart of God?

Glance back at John 1:14 at the top of the page. What does it mean to say Jesus was "full of grace and truth"?

Why are both necessary?

Grace and Truth

The text says Jesus is full of both grace and truth. This is excellent news for sinners. Why? Because truth without grace is cruel. On the other hand, grace without truth allows people to flounder in their sin and remain separated from God. But grace and truth says: "You have a sin problem that separates you from God—but by my grace I've made a way for you to be reconciled to the Father." Paul wrote,

> *For by grace you have been saved through faith. And*
> *this is not your own doing; it is the gift of God, not*
> *a result of works, so that no one may boast.*
> **EPHESIANS 2:8-9**

In a sense, the gospel is bad news before it's good news. The bad news is all people have a sin problem and have fallen short of the glory of God (Rom. 3:23). Without Christ, there's nothing we can do to improve our standing before God. The good news is that God is full of grace, and we can be saved by grace through faith. And God's grace isn't a one-time offering—He gives grace upon grace—it includes our salvation, but it doesn't stop there (John 1:16). God's grace is an inexhaustible well that will never run dry.

Why do you think many of us feel more comfortable attempting to earn God's favor rather than freely accepting the grace He offers?

Do you struggle with accepting God's grace? Explain why you feel the way you do.

If we have been saved by grace, why is boasting inappropriate in the life of a believer?

Born in the Likeness of Men

*Have this mind among yourselves, which is yours in Christ Jesus,
who, though he was in the form of God, did not count equality
with God a thing to be grasped, but emptied himself, by taking
the form of a servant, being born in the likeness of men. And
being found in human form, he humbled himself by becoming
obedient to the point of death, even death on a cross.*
PHILIPPIANS 2:5-8

What stands out to you in these verses?

How do you see evidence of Jesus' grace to us in these verses?

What did it cost Jesus to be born in the likeness of men?

It was costly for Jesus to put on flesh and dwell among us. By taking on flesh, the
all-powerful King of the Universe became a man from an obscure town called
Nazareth (John 1:46). Jesus came to seek and save the lost (Luke 19:10). Yet, He
was despised and rejected by those He came to save. During His time on earth,
He was familiar with sorrow and grief (Isa. 53:3). Ultimately, His mission led Him to
a torturous death on a Roman cross (John 19:28-30) where He died for those who
had despised and rejected Him. Jesus embodied grace upon grace.

> *Close your time today in prayer by giving thanks to God that
> He is full of both grace and truth. Ask God to reveal if you
> have a scarcity mindset, and ask Him to renew your thoughts
> until you see that you serve a God who is full of grace.*

Personal Study 2
FROM HIS FULLNESS

For from his fullness we have all received, grace upon grace.
JOHN 1:16

You're probably familiar with the analogy that some people look at a glass of water and see it as half full, and others look at it and see it as half empty. How we mentally frame things tells us a lot about what we believe. As Christians, our goal is to align our thinking with the truths found in God's Word.

Generally speaking, do you tend to see a glass as half full or half empty? What are the pros and cons of seeing things the way you do?

According to the passage above, from Jesus' fullness we have all received grace upon grace. What did John mean by Jesus' fullness?

In what areas of your life are you in need of the fullness of God?

Bringing to mind and recalling various ways that God has shown His grace in our lives stirs our faith and helps us to see He will show us grace for our future needs. Jesus secured our salvation by His sacrifice at Calvary. Paul wrote, "He who did not spare his own Son but gave him up for us all, how will he not also with him graciously give us all things?" (Rom. 8:32). In other words, since God has already offered us the ultimate gift in Jesus—He will undoubtedly continue to give us everything else we need in the future.

Do you ever struggle worrying about whether or not God will provide the grace you need? If so, what specific areas are you concerned about?

What role does prayer play in presenting your worries to God?

On a scale of 1 to 10, how would you rate your prayer life?

Think for a moment about your history with God. List several ways He has proved Himself faithful.

Grace to Help

Let us then with confidence draw near to the throne of grace, that we may receive mercy and find grace to help in time of need.
HEBREWS 4:16

According to the text above, what do we receive when we draw near to the throne of grace? How do we take advantage of this?

Why do we tend to place limits on the amount of mercy and grace we can receive from Jesus? Why is this attitude unbiblical?

The author of the Book of Hebrews extends an astounding invitation by encouraging readers to approach the throne of grace with confidence. If you are a child of God, you don't have to come timidly to the throne. While we should certainly approach God with reverence and respect, we can simultaneously come with confidence. The Bible teaches that we can come to the throne of God and receive mercy and grace in our time of need, but we must approach the throne to ask. Prayer is a privilege that we neglect at our own peril.

What prevents you from taking your needs to God in prayer?

After this week's study, do you think you have a scarcity mentality or an abundance mentality? Why do you feel the way you do?

Which areas in your thought life do you need to realign with the truths found in God's Word? What passages speak to those issues?

Eugene Peterson's translation of John 1:14 captures the grace and generosity of Christ:

The Word became flesh and blood, and moved into the neighborhood. We saw the glory with our own eyes, the one-of-a-kind glory, like Father, like Son, Generous inside and out, true from start to finish.
JOHN 1:14 (MSG)

Close your time in prayer giving thanks to God for the grace He has shown in your life. Ask Him to empower you to be someone who is quick to show grace to others.

The Word and the Witness

GROUP STUDY

Start
Welcome everyone to session 4.

When you meet someone for the first time, what introductory information do you share about yourself?

If you had to pick one or two phrases to describe who you are as a person, what would they be?

At some point, we all wrestle with who we are as individuals. Many of us assume we find out who we are by looking within—but that's not the case. If we want to find out who we are as human beings, we have to look at ourselves in view of the God who created us.

Why do you think we learn more about ourselves as we grow in our understanding of God?

To prepare for video session 4, pray that God will help each person understand and apply this truth:

Like John the Baptist, we are able to know who we are and who we are not because we know who Jesus is.

Watch

*Use the space below to take notes
while you watch video session 4.*

Discuss

*Use the following questions to guide
your discussion of the video.*

1. Pastor J. T. said, "To be an ideal witness of Christ, to learn what it looks like to grow and testify to God's work in our lives, you have to know three things: You have to know who you're not, you have to know who you are, and you can only know those two things because you know who Jesus is." Why do we have to know who Jesus is before we can make an accurate estimation of who we are?

2. In what ways was John the Baptist a good example of these qualities?

3. Why is it important to know who you aren't? How does knowing who we aren't relieve the burdens we've placed on ourselves?

4. How might culture, family members, friends, and coworkers pressure us to be someone we aren't? Can you think of any examples?

5. Pastor J. T. said, "Anxiety, fear, and depression riddle our lives because we are trying to live a life that we simply can't live with expectations that we will never live up to." In what ways can you relate to this in your own life?

6. Tell about a time when you realized you were trying to be someone you aren't or attempting to fill a role you couldn't fill. How did it turn out?

7. In John 1:20, John the Baptist said, "I am not the Christ." Why would it be freeing to acknowledge who we are and who we aren't?

8. Pastor J. T. said, "Christians often do not realize who they are in Jesus' eyes." In your experience, how have you found this to be true?

PRAYER REQUESTS

FAMILY DISCIPLESHIP

Like John the Baptist, we are able to know who we are and who we are not because we know who Jesus is.

If you need to, reword this week's truth so that your whole family can understand it.

■ **TIME:** Read John 1:19-28. Encourage children to read the Scripture if they're able. Take turns reading the verses out loud. Point out that John the Baptist said, "I am not the Christ" (1:20). Explain that there is only one God, and we are not Him. Ask them to give examples of why it's good news that God is in control and human beings are not.

■ **MOMENTS:** Throughout the week help children to define who they are in relation to God. For instance, when we approach God in prayer we are demonstrating that we are sons and daughters of the King but when we help other people show that we are God's servants. Explain that since God is their Creator—the more they grow in their knowledge and understanding of God—the more they will know about themselves.

■ **MILESTONES:** Talk to your children about the unique ways God has created them. Point out their strengths, skills, and talents and explain that God has gifted them. Explain that as children of God, they have opportunities to use the gifts for His glory. Schedule a time when your child can use his or her gifts to serve. For instance, an older child might help a younger child with homework. A younger child might make a card to encourage someone who is sick.

I AM NOT THE CHRIST

In session 2, we introduced John the Baptist. This session, we'll be taking a more detailed look at John and his ministry. From John the Baptist, we can learn what it means to be a witness for Christ in a world of chaos and confusion.

Read John 1:19-28.

How would you describe John's response when the priests and Levites questioned him? (vv. 19-23).

Why did John define himself in relation to Jesus? (v. 23)

What can we learn from John the Baptist about being a witness for Christ?

People love to draw attention to themselves. We see it on TV, on social media, in our workplaces, and we undoubtedly know people who are doing everything they can to climb the social ladder. When John the Baptist began his ministry, it didn't take long before crowds were gathering to hear him preach (Matt. 3:5). Jewish authorities were curious about who he was, so they sent the priests and Levites to inquire (1:19). Under the scrutiny, John refused to promote himself. Instead, he denied that he was the Christ and said his reason for coming was to point people to Jesus (1:20).

What evidence do you see in the text that John knew who he was but also who he wasn't?

How did John demonstrate humility?

Why is humility an essential character trait for a Christ-follower?

A Voice Crying in the Wilderness

He said, "I am the voice of one crying out in the wilderness, 'Make straight the way of the Lord,' as the prophet Isaiah said."
JOHN 1:23

John the Baptist knew who he wasn't, and he knew who he was, all because he knew who Jesus was. What does it look like to be an ideal witness of Christ, to learn what it looks like to grow and testify to God's work in our lives? You have to know three things: You have to know who you're not, you have to know who you are, and you can only know those two things because you know who Jesus is.

Scripture teaches we were created by Jesus and for Jesus (John 1:3; Col. 1:16). With that in mind, why is it impossible to know who we are apart from Christ?

Name some of the outside sources we look to other than God to define who we are. Why do they lead to an inaccurate estimation about who we are and why we are here?

Growing in Knowledge of God

John Calvin opened up his most famous work, *Institutes of the Christian Religion*, with this phrase. He said, "Nearly all the wisdom we possess, that is to say, true and sound wisdom, consists of two parts: the knowledge of God and of ourselves." In other words, Calvin is saying, "If you want to grow as a disciple of Jesus, if you want to know what it looks like to represent and be a disciple of Jesus, you must grow in a knowledge of God."[1]

On a day-to-day basis, how do you grow in your knowledge of God?

List a couple of new things you've learned or been reminded of about God since beginning this study.

How has this growing knowledge of God provided additional insight into your own heart and character?

John the Baptist understood who Jesus was, and he knew his role was to prepare the hearts and minds of the people for His coming (John 1:23). John's knowledge about Christ motivated him to make Jesus' mission his own. One of the remarkable things about growing in our knowledge about God is the more we know about Him, the more we will love Him. As we study the Scriptures, we grow in our adoration, affection, and love of Jesus Christ, and we align our identity with His.

> *Close your time in prayer by giving thanks for the opportunity to grow in our relationship with Jesus through the study of the Scriptures. Ask God to reveal Himself to you in increasing measure.*

1. https://www.placefortruth.org/blog/calvins-theology-nearly-all-wisdom-we-possess.

Personal Study 2
I AM NOT WORTHY

John answered them, "I baptize with water, but among you stands one you do not know, even he who comes after me, the strap of whose sandal I am not worthy to untie."
JOHN 1:26-27

John the Baptist is often remembered for his humility. Keep in mind, John was a flesh and blood human being and therefore prone to pride and self-promotion along with the rest of humanity. When John's ministry began, and his preaching started to draw crowds, there must have been some temptation to bask in the spotlight (Matt. 3:4-6) but nothing in the Scriptures suggests he did.

How would you describe what it looks like to be humble?

How frequently do you see humility displayed in those around you? How about in our culture?

Name a few people you can think of who you consider to be humble. What stands out about them?

In the first-century, speculation about the coming Messiah abounded, so it's not surprising that the authorities questioned John about his identity (1: 19). Yet, John was quick to tell them he was not the Christ (1:20). He also denied being Elijah (1:21). John the Baptist is giving us a model. In essence, John was saying: "I'm not the Christ. Don't place those expectations on me. I'm not a supernatural miracle-worker like Elijah. Don't place those expectations upon me either. I am not the Prophet. I'm simply a voice in the wilderness."

Because John knew who he was, he understood his role. When asked why he was baptizing, he said:

I baptize with water, but among you stands one you
do not know, even he who comes after me, the strap
of whose sandal I am not worthy to untie.
JOHN 1:26-27

John the Baptist was strange and misunderstood. However, he knew who Jesus was while the religious elite didn't have a clue. John's knowledge of Jesus prompted him to say he wasn't worthy to tie His sandals (1:27). Genuine self-knowledge should lead us to deeper awareness of our brokenness and lead us to humility. Therefore, self-exploration should lead us to our need for Christ.

Why is it impossible to have a close relationship with Jesus and remain self-absorbed and boastful?

Why does a close relationship with Jesus foster humility?

Everyone has areas of weakness. In what specific areas are you prone to struggle with humility?

Life is about Jesus, not about us. John understood that Jesus was on the ultimate mission and he was called to play a supporting role. The gospel is good news, not because of who we are but because of who Jesus is. To be sure, we find our place in relation to Him. But Jesus is the focal point and everyone else plays a supporting role. What's extraordinary though, is John was reflecting the humility of Christ.

Christ's Example

Read Philippians 2:3-11.

According to verse 3, what motives are we to avoid when we do something?

How is it possible to do something good with a poor motive? Can you think of an example?

Glance back at verses 5-7. What are some of the specific ways Jesus demonstrated humility?

How can you, like John the Baptist, model the humility of Jesus?

The whole purpose of Jesus' humility, servanthood, and sacrifice was for the glory of God. The same will be true for us. The closer we get to Jesus, the more aware we will become of how much grace we have received. The apostle Paul asked, "What do you have that you did not receive?" (1 Cor. 4:7). If we answer that question honestly, the only appropriate response will be humility.

> *Close your time giving thanks to God for Jesus' example of humility, servanthood, and sacrifice. Ask God to reveal areas where you lack humility. Pray you will be in such close fellowship with Jesus that humility will be the byproduct of your relationship with Him.*

Behold the Lamb

GROUP STUDY

Start
Welcome everyone to session 5.

Sin is an unpopular topic in today's culture. Why do you think that is?

How would you describe the concept of sin to a child?

Earlier in this study, we discussed that we are created "by Jesus and for Jesus" (Col. 1:16). But the Bible teaches that because of our sinful nature, we have been separated from God. Our sin nature includes our behavior, but it goes even deeper than that—sin has corrupted the nature of our hearts. God knew there was nothing we could do to change ourselves so He did so by sending His Son to save us from our sins.

Our personal sins have the potential to impact other people. Can you think of times when this is the case?

To prepare for video session 5, pray that God will help each person understand and apply this truth:

Jesus is the Lamb of God who will defeat all sin.

Watch

Use the space below to take notes
while you watch video session 5.

Video sessions available at lifeway.com/johnbiblestudy

Discuss

*Use the following questions to guide
your discussion of the video.*

1. Read Colossians 1:21-22. In this passage, Paul says before receiving Christ's salvation, we were all "alienated and hostile in mind, doing evil deeds." Why did it take Jesus coming in the flesh to reconcile us to God?

2. Sometimes we tend to avoid the word *sin* and instead say things like "failures, short-comings, or poor choices." Why is it difficult to call sin for what it is? What do we miss by refusing to identify sin specifically?

3. At what point did you realize you had a sin problem that separated you from God? What led up to this realization?

4. What are common ways we attempt to justify our sins? Why is this foolish?

5. Pastor Matt said, "To bring morality to God as though that's a currency that He accepts is a fool's errand because it's not just not accepted; it's called, in the Bible, filthy rags." Why do we attempt to bring our good works to God? Why can this not save us?

6. When John the Baptist saw Jesus, he said, "Behold, the Lamb of God who takes away the sins of the world" (John 1:29). Why is Jesus the only One capable of dealing with our sin problem?

7. Last session we talked about the fact that in Christ, "we have all received, grace upon grace" (John 1: 16). How is that demonstrated in Jesus' willingness to forgive past, present, and future sins?

8. Pastor Matt asked, "What stirs your affections for Jesus Christ, and what robs you of those affections?" How would you answer that question?

PRAYER REQUESTS

FAMILY DISCIPLESHIP

Jesus is the Lamb of God who will defeat all sin.

If you need to, reword this week's truth so that your whole family can understand it.

■ **TIME:** Read John 1:29-34. Encourage children to read the Scripture if they're able. Take turns reading the verses out loud. Emphasize that John the Baptist said, "Behold, the Lamb of God who takes away the sin of the world (1:29). Explain that we all sin and our sin separates us from God. Tell them that God loves us so much that He sent Jesus into the world to defeat sin and reconcile us to God.

■ **MOMENTS:** Encourage children to be open and share the ways they sin and fall short of God's glory. Depending on their age, examples might include disobeying their parents, acting unkindly toward their siblings, or an unwillingness to share or cooperate with friends. Explain that all of us sin but that if we confess our sins to God and ask for His forgiveness, He will forgive us.

■ **MILESTONES:** Acknowledge the anniversary date of when your child became a Christian. Talk about how God sent Jesus to defeat sin. Bring up areas of sin you used to struggle with but by God's grace He has equipped you to defeat. Encourage children to talk about areas they struggle with and discuss how, with God's help, they can overcome areas of weakness.

BEHOLD THE LAMB OF GOD

We've talked about the fact that John the Baptist was a man with characteristics that made him a powerful example of what it looks like to follow Jesus. As a prophet, his role was to prepare people's hearts and minds for Jesus' coming. In today's lesson, we'll see how John responds when he sees Jesus approaching.

Read John 1:29-34.

Why is it significant that John referred to Jesus as the Lamb of God? Why would this have been important to those who heard?

Why is it noteworthy that John the Baptist called Jesus "the Lamb" instead of "a lamb"?

John said Jesus' reason for coming was to "take away the sins of the world." With this in mind, why is it foolish to attempt to minimize or hide our sins from Jesus?

In our current place in history, the phrase, "Lamb of God" doesn't resonate in the same way it did when John the Baptist first spoke those words. To the Jews who heard those words, "the lamb" meant everything. The title "Lamb of God" derives from the theme of Passover (Ex. 12; 29) and the Suffering Servant passages in the Book of Isaiah:

He was oppressed, and he was afflicted,
yet he opened not his mouth;
like a lamb that is led to the slaughter,
and like a sheep that before its shearers is silent,
so he opened not his mouth.
ISAIAH 53:7

How did this prophecy of Christ written by the prophet Isaiah come to fruition in Jesus' life and ministry? Give specific examples.

In the Old Testament, there had to be a shedding of blood for the covering of sins, which was done through sacrificing animals. How does Jesus fill this sacrificial role for all who place their faith in Him?

The Iniquity of Us All

In the Old Testament, animal sacrifices had to be offered over and over again. Jesus came to deal with sin once and for all. It's significant that John the Baptist didn't refer to Jesus as "a lamb of God" but "the Lamb of God." Jesus was the one who God appointed to be the final sacrifice for sin. Although we were the guilty party, God sent Jesus to die in our place. The prophets Isaiah said,

All we like sheep have gone astray; we have turned—every one—
to his own way; and the LORD has laid on him the iniquity of us all.
ISAIAH 53:6

How do these passages from Isaiah inform your thinking about Jesus as "the Lamb of God?"

Think about the fact that Jesus willingly took on the sins of humankind— including yours. What emotions does that provoke in you?

The author of the Book of Hebrews wrote, "For it is impossible for the blood of bulls and goats to take away sins" (Heb. 10:4). There's an old saying, "God helps those who help themselves." However, nothing could be further from the truth. Jesus came to do what we could not do for ourselves. We could not eliminate our sin problem, and the animal sacrifices of the Old Testament didn't have the power to save us from our sins. Only Jesus could save us, and He did. Hebrews says:

> *But when Christ had offered for all time a single sacrifice for sins, he sat down at the right hand of God, waiting from that time until his enemies should be made a footstool for his feet.*
> **HEBREWS 10:12-13**

Jesus made a once and for all sacrifice for our sins—but it was costly. How does considering the great cost of grace help you better appreciate the grace you have received?

Why should these realities motivate a posture of humility in us?

Close your time in prayer by confessing your sins to God and asking for forgiveness. Give thanks that because of Jesus' sacrifice you can be reconciled to God.

Personal Study 2
REMAIN AND ABIDE

And John bore witness: "I saw the Spirit descend from heaven like a dove, and it remained on him.
JOHN 1:32

Jesus came not only to take away the sins of the world (past tense), His work also continues. John the Baptist could've said "Behold, the Lamb of God who's *continuing* to take away the sins of the world." Not only is this a present and ongoing action, but so is the abiding power of the Holy Spirit. The text above says the Spirit remained on Jesus. Likewise, if we are children of God, the Holy Spirit remains on us (Rom. 8:9). In this way, we begin to get a sense of what the Christian life is. Receiving eternal life and the forgiveness of our sins is only the starting point of our life with Jesus.

> **Do you know anyone who became a Christian and then exhibited no discernible spiritual growth? Why is this an inaccurate picture of what it means to follow Christ?**

> **What changes about our lives when we continue to remain in Jesus?**

Jesus came to take away the sins of the world but seeking His forgiveness for our sins is the launching point and not the final destination. God intends for His people to abide in Jesus, and learn what it means to experience life to the fullest. Jesus said, "The thief comes only to steal and kill and destroy. I came that they may have life and have it abundantly" (John 10:10). Abiding in Jesus doesn't mean we don't have problems—Jesus warned that we should expect them (John 16:33). But if we abide in Christ, we can anticipate His peace, provision, and joy regardless of our circumstances.

What Does it Mean to Abide?

Read John 15:4-11.

Glance back at verse 4. What metaphor does Jesus use? What does this teach us about life with Christ?

What does it look like to abide in Jesus on a daily basis?

What are some of the common obstacles you face that prevent you from abiding in Christ?

Jesus was a master teacher and He often communicated by using analogies that were well-known to His audience. In an agrarian society, it's not surprising that He spoke about agriculture and used the example of a vine and branch. Jesus' teaching style often included using familiar examples to teach unfamiliar spiritual truths. On it's own, a branch doesn't possess what it needs to survive—it relies on the vine to supply the resources it needs to grow and flourish. In the same way, apart from Christ, God's people don't have what it takes to live the Christian life— we must remain closely connected to Jesus—relying on Him to bear fruit.

Have you experienced a time of abiding in Christ and the you got sidetracked? What differences do you notice between times of abiding compared to when you're not?

Glance back at verse 5. According to Jesus, when it comes to our spiritual life, how much can we accomplish without Him? Is this hard for you to accept? Why or why not?

Christ promises that those who abide in Him will bear fruit. What does it look like for you to bear fruit?

The apostle Paul describes the fruit of the Spirit this way:

> *But the fruit of the Spirit is love, joy, peace, patience,*
> *kindness, goodness, faithfulness, gentleness,*
> *self-control; against such things there is no law.*
> **GALATIANS 5:22-23**

How would your life be different if you prioritized abiding in Jesus above everything else?

What steps can you take to make abiding in Jesus a priority in your weekly rhythms?

Close your time today asking Jesus to help you abide in Him. Give thanks to God that because of His grace He's given you the opportunity to know and fellowship with Him.

Called to Follow

GROUP STUDY

Start
Welcome everyone to session 6.

What details do you notice when you receive a printed invitation?

How do you decide if you will accept or decline an invitation?

Invitations are fun to receive—they might come in the form of a birthday party, wedding, family gathering, work event, dinner party, or any manner of social gathering. Invitations vary, but they have common characteristics that communicate who, what, when, where, and why. In this session, we'll see that Jesus issues an invitation for us to follow Him, and He invites us to "Come and see" (John 1:39).

If you were speaking to someone unfamiliar with Christianity, what would you tell them about following Jesus?

To prepare for video session 6, pray that God will help each person understand and apply this truth:

> Jesus continues to draw followers to Himself in the same ways He drew His first disciples.

Watch

*Use the space below to take notes
while you watch video session 6.*

Discuss
*Use the following questions to guide
your discussion of the video.*

1.   How would you describe the difference between believing Jesus exists and following Him as Lord? How do people get the two confused?

2.   Jesus asked two disciples of John the Baptist, "What are you seeking?" (John 1:38). Why is this an important question for all of us?

3.   Do you think people have unrealistic expectations of what it looks like to follow Jesus? Why or why not? If so, explain why you think that's the case.

4.   What is something you've learned since following Jesus that could only be known by following Him?

5.   Pastor Matt said, "To this day, Jesus gathers to Himself men and women to follow Him through the proclamation of His Word. Where it is proclaimed and people hear it and understand it, they will follow Him." How should this reality motivate preaching and evangelism?

6.   Name a few of the ways your life is different because you follow Jesus.

7.   For you, what are the most enjoyable aspects of being a Christ-follower? What would you say is the most challenging?

8.   What role have fellow-believers played as you have followed Jesus? How would things be different without them?

9.   Who might you invite to come and follow Jesus alongside you?

PRAYER REQUESTS

FAMILY DISCIPLESHIP

Jesus continues to draw followers to Himself in the same ways He drew His first disciples.

Reword this week's truth so that your whole family can understand it.

■ **TIME:** Read John 1:35-51. Encourage children to read the Scripture if they're able. Take turns reading the verses out loud. Point out the passage that says, "The next day Jesus decided to go to Galilee. He found Philip and said to him, 'Follow me'" (John 1:43). Explain that Jesus invites people to follow Him as Lord. Encourage them to ask questions about what that means.

■ **MOMENTS:** Throughout the week, point out ordinary events in your life that happen because you follow Jesus. Examples might include Bible-reading, praying before meals, asking God for help in specific areas of life, giving thanks, and worshiping at church. Explain that following Jesus impacts every aspect of life but is most often seen in our day-to-day living.

■ **MILESTONES:** Spend time encouraging children to talk about what they have learned since they started following Jesus. Point out areas where you see that they have grown or matured. Encourage them by identifying areas where you see them thriving. Ask them to verbalize in their own words how their life is influenced because they follow Christ.

WHAT ARE YOU SEEKING?

Since the beginning of Jesus' ministry people have been confused and conflicted about His identity. In the first-century, Messianic speculation ran rampant and numerous theories about His identity circulated widely. When John the Baptist came face-to-face with Jesus he was quick to proclaim who Jesus was and said, "Behold, the Lamb of God!" (John 1:36). Jesus provoked varied responses from people and in this biblical account two disciples of John followed Jesus:

> *The two disciples heard him say this, and they followed Jesus. Jesus turned and saw them following and said to them, "What are you seeking?" And they said to him, "Rabbi" (which means Teacher), "where are you staying?" He said to them, "Come and you will see." So they came and saw where he was staying, and they stayed with him that day, for it was about the tenth hour.*
> **JOHN 1:37-39**

What did Jesus ask the men? Why is this a question we all have to answer?

The two men asked Jesus where He was staying. How did Jesus respond? What does Jesus' response tell us about His nature?

Notice, Jesus asked the two men, "What are you seeking?" People come to Jesus for a variety of reasons, but would-be followers of Jesus need to count the cost of discipleship. Jesus never sugarcoated what it might cost to follow Him. In Luke's Gospel, a potential Christ-follower said he'd follow Jesus and Jesus warned that if he did so he might wind up homeless: "And Jesus said to him, 'Foxes have holes, and birds of the air have nests, but the Son of Man has nowhere to lay his head'" (Luke 9:58). Jesus never promised that following Him would be easy. On the contrary, He told His followers to expect opposition (John 15:18-25).

Think for a moment about your relationship with Jesus. What are you seeking? Describe the kind of relationship you want with Him.

Are you willing to follow Jesus on His terms? Why or why not?

What evidence have you seen that following Jesus is worth the cost?

Come and You Will See

When the two men asked Jesus where He was staying He said, "Come and you will see" (John 1:39). The men took Jesus up on His invitation and spent the day with Him. During the time of Jesus' earthly ministry, teaching included learning from a rabbi's spoken words—but it wasn't limited to verbal teaching. Disciples followed a rabbi or teacher and learned from his daily habits and lifestyle. Jesus' intention is never for His followers to merely know about Him—He invites us into a lifestyle of knowing Him.

What is the difference between knowing about someone and truly knowing them?

Think about the people you know the best. How did you get to know them well?

What are some barriers that prevent you from getting to know someone? What are the main things that prevent you from growing in your relationship with Jesus?

Why do we sometimes confuse knowing about Jesus for actually knowing Jesus?

How is it possible for modern-day believers to know Jesus well?

Jesus' invitation to follow Him isn't a lifetime offer of dead religion. Jesus invites us into a living and thriving relationship. Since this is possible we'd be fools to settle for anything less. As believers today, we follow Christ by studying and obeying the Scriptures, cultivating a lifestyle of devoted prayer, and being active members of a biblical community in a local church. There's a massive difference between believing Jesus exists and following Him as Lord. And there's a difference between knowing about Jesus and following Him so closely we recognize His voice. Jesus said, "My sheep hear my voice, and I know them, and they follow me. I give them eternal life, and they will never perish, and no one will snatch them out of my hand" (John 10:27-28).

> *Close your time today by telling Jesus what you are seeking from Him. Tell Him the kind of relationship you want to have. Ask Him to teach you to follow so closely that you easily recognize His voice among the others.*

Personal Study 2
FOLLOW ME

The next day Jesus decided to go to Galilee. He found Philip and said to him, "Follow me."
JOHN 1:43

In the first century, it was customary for a disciple to take interest in a rabbi and choose to follow him. The relationship depended on the disciple's motivation to attach himself to a rabbi's ministry. Jesus differed in His approach by taking the initiative and extending an invitation. He said to Philip, "Follow me" (1:43). This approach reflects the goal of Jesus' mission. Luke said, "For the Son of Man came to seek and to save the lost" (Luke 19:10).

Why is it significant that Jesus initiates relationships with His disciples?

If Jesus, initiates the relationship, what responsibility do we have to take? Explain.

The Bible makes it clear that Jesus initiates relationships and issues an invitation for people to follow Him. But a response is required on our part. To ignore Jesus' invitation is the equivalent of refusing Him. In Luke's Gospel, Jesus reveals what it looks like to follow Him:

> *And he said to all, "If anyone would come after me, let him deny himself and take up his cross daily and follow me. For whoever would save his life will lose it, but whoever loses his life for my sake will save it. For what does it profit a man if he gains the whole world and loses or forfeits himself?*
> **LUKE 9:23-25**

What do you think Jesus meant when He said His followers are to "deny themselves?" How does this message differ from what we routinely hear in our culture?

For the first disciples, there was a significant risk in following Jesus. What risks are there today?

How do the risks in America differ from what Christians experience in other parts of the world?

Following Jesus requires self-denial because we are no longer living for ourselves and our agenda. Christ-followers are focused on Jesus and an agenda that serves the kingdom of God. Jesus said a Christ-follower is to "take up his cross daily and follow me" (v. 23). In Roman culture, the cross was the most excruciating form of execution. So by saying that we are to "take up our cross," Jesus was saying we must be willing to be subjected to painful circumstances because of our allegiance to Him.

What did Jesus mean when He said, "For whoever would save his life will lose it, but whoever loses his life for my sake will save it" (v. 24)?

How is it possible to gain the whole world and lose yourself? (v. 25).

In all four Gospels, there's a common theme that communicates a Christ-follower must lose his life to save it (John 12:25; Luke 14:26-27, 17:33; Mt. 10:38-39, 16:24-25; Mark 8:34-35). The point is, Christians must abandon their devotion to this broken world and go all in for Christ and His mission. No matter how much wealth, privilege, success, or esteem is gained in this lifetime; a person will find himself eternally bankrupt if he dies apart from Christ.

Notice that Jesus said we are to take up our cross "daily." Do you think dying to self is a one-time decision or something we have to choose every morning? Explain your answer.

Dying to self isn't something we can do in our own power. Why do we have to rely on Jesus to live the kind of life He commands?

What are common reasons people hold out from going "all in" following Jesus?

In your experience, why is following Jesus worth the cost?

Close your time today by asking God to empower you to live the kind of life that John's Gospel describes. Tell Him your fears and reservations. Ask Him for the type of relationship with Jesus that makes the costs more than worth it.

SESSION 7

New Wine

GROUP STUDY

Start

Welcome everyone to session 7.

Have you experienced a time when you stopped an old way of doing something and implemented a new plan? If so, what happened?

What are the challenges that come with a new way of doing things?

This session, we'll study Jesus' first miracle at a wedding in Cana. This first miracle—which John refers to as a "sign"—represents the reality that the old way had passed and a new way had come (John 2:11). New beginnings are exciting, but there's always a temptation to fall back into familiar patterns and old habits.

Have you ever asked why something was done a certain way and heard the response, "Because that's how we've always done it." Why is this a poor reason?

To prepare for video session 7, pray that God will help each person understand and apply this truth:

> The inaugural sign of Jesus' ministry reminds us that the old has passed away and the new has come.

Watch

*Use the space below to take notes
while you watch video session 7.*

Discuss

*Use the following questions to guide
your discussion of the video.*

1. How does our vertical relationship with Christ influence our horizontal relationship with others?

2. Read Matthew 20:25-28. How does this passage differ from the message of the "me culture" we live in?

3. Pastor Matt said, "If you pay attention to your frustrations and agitations, they are almost always tied to thinking life is about you." How have you experienced this to be true?

4. Pastor Matt discussed that Christians are to be "marked by having a servant's heart." What does having a servant's heart look like? How does this mentality differ from our culture?

5. Who do you know who has a servant's heart? What makes them stand out from their peers?

6. What are some of the reasons people might be hesitant to take on the role of a servant? Are these reasons legitimate? Why or why not?

7. Paul wrote, "So then, as we have opportunity, let us do good to everyone, and especially to those who are of the household of faith" (Gal. 6:10). How would life be different if every Christ-follower was committed to doing good to everyone at every opportunity? What might change?

8. How might Christians develop a reputation for doing good to everyone?

9. Jesus' first miracle conveyed the reality that the old had passed away, and a new way in Christ had come. What are some "old ways" you are holding to despite having a new life in Christ?

PRAYER REQUESTS

FAMILY DISCIPLESHIP

The inaugural sign of Jesus' ministry reminds us the old has passed away and the new has come.

If you need to, reword this week's truth so that your whole family can understand it.

■ **TIME:** Read John 2:1-12. Encourage children to read the Scripture if they're able. Take turns reading the verses out loud. Explain that Jesus got invited to a wedding and His mother told Him the hosts ran out of wine. In this culture, hospitality was important and running out of food or drink was embarrassing. Explain that Jesus performed His first miracle at the wedding in Cana to illustrate that a new way had come.

■ **MOMENTS:** During dinner time, encourage children to share reasons why their life is different because Jesus has come. Examples might include that we have been forgiven for our sins, are never alone, that we have a different standard of how to live, and that we have God's strength in us. Explain that when Jesus is at the center of our life the old ways of doing things have passed and we are a new person in Christ with a new way of living (2 Cor. 5:17).

■ **MILESTONES:** Depending on their age, encourage children to think back to when they first learned about Jesus. What significant events have taken place since then? How is their life different now? Ask them to share ways they have changed and grown in their faith.

Personal Study 1
THE WEDDING AT CANA

Read John 2:1-12.

Throughout his Gospel, John refers to Jesus' miracles as "signs." John wanted to communicate that Jesus didn't perform miracles just because He was able. Rather, Jesus was pointing onlookers to something greater. Jesus' miracles demonstrated He had been sent by the Father. His signs authenticated His identity as the Messiah they'd been anticipating (Luke 7:22).

In this passage, we find Jesus at a wedding. What does it tell us about Jesus that He was invited and attended social gatherings?

How would you describe Jesus' response when Mary tells Him the wine had run out?

Why would Jesus resist Mary? What did Jesus mean when He said His hour had not yet come?

In the Middle East, hospitality was, and still is, taken seriously. Running out of wine would've embarrassed the newly married couple. Mary rushed to Jesus to solve the problem and spare the wedding party from public ridicule. Jesus' terse response to Mary may seem out of character, but it signaled a turning point. This was Jesus' first miracle. He was stepping out in ministry. Mary, and everyone else's request are less important than the Father's plan. "My hour" refers to the hour of Jesus' glorification where His identity would be fully revealed. The fact that Jesus ultimately did what Mary asked, shows His initial response was a statement of priority rather than a rejection of Mary's request.

Why should we seek to prioritize our obedience to the Father over the wishes of others?

Have you ever obeyed God and disappointed a family member or friend because of your obedience? If so, what did you learn?

Glance back at verse 5. How did Mary respond to Jesus? What can we learn from her?

A New Way

Look at verse six, what were the water vessels at the wedding used for? Why is it significant that Jesus uses these vessels to make wine?

For the Jews of this day, any moral or physical blemish made one unclean and unfit to be in the presence of God until there was a rite or ritual of ceremonial cleaning that restored fellowship with God. Jesus, in this act of transforming water and purification jars into wine, is replacing that old model with something new. Jesus began His ministry with a sign that displayed His glory and drew onlookers to see that Jesus and the new kingdom had arrived.

How did the disciples respond to Jesus' signs (v. 11)? How should we respond to Jesus' work in our own lives?

John makes it clear that Jesus' disciples saw His miracle and came to faith in Him (2:11). For a modern audience, it's important to realize that all of Jesus' "signs" were designed to point to His power and affirm His divinity.

Why do new ways of doing things tend to throw us off balance?

How might we embrace the new work Jesus is trying to do in and through us?

Seeing the new work of Jesus should always result in belief and new life. Jesus' ministry, and this miracle specifically, had brought a new era of redemption history where what was coming would be exceedingly better than what came before. The old had passed and the new had come. Jesus announced a new way founded in His redemptive work (John 14:6).

> *Close your time giving thanks to God that the old has passed and the new has come.*

Personal Study 2

A NEW CREATION

Read 2 Corinthians 5:17-21.

Jesus didn't just come to change the sacrificial system and purification rites of the Old Testament—Jesus came to change the hearts and minds of people and to give us a new nature. Our relationship with Jesus changes us and makes us a new creation. As we are changed by Jesus, our relationship with Him changes our relationship with other people.

Glance back at verse 17. What is true of everyone who is "in Christ?"

How has God reconciled us to Himself through Christ?

In this passage, Paul refers to God's people as "ambassadors for Christ." What does it mean to be an ambassador for Christ?

A New Role

An ambassador is a diplomat who represents and advocates for the interest of a nation or an organization. An ambassador for Christ is a citizen of the kingdom of heaven who uses their Spirit-given abilities to advocate for Christ. At first glace, this role may seem intimidating. But before we get stressed, we have to remember that a Christian lives out of the overflow of abiding in Jesus. We aren't called to be superhuman—we are called to abide in Jesus and trust Him to equip us to do what we can't accomplish in our own strength. Success in our role is dependent on Jesus, not on our skill.

List a few ways you can be an "ambassador for Christ" in your circle of influence.

How does your relationship with Jesus influence your other relationships?

Name a few people whose lives are better because of your relationship with Christ.

Being an ambassador is not a call to be unnaturally religious. God takes our striving out of our hands by requiring that we come to Him and abide with Him. Abiding in Jesus, knowing Jesus, loving Jesus, and growing in intimacy with Jesus transforms us in such a way that there is a kindness, life, and joy in us that other people are naturally drawn to and want to be around.

How would you describe the difference between being "unnaturally religious" and a person who abides in Jesus?

Paul said, "we are ministers of reconciliation" (2 Cor. 5:18). What does that mean for us and our relationships?

A New Motive

Obedience to God and service to others are two markers of someone who has been reconciled to God and taken on the role of an ambassador for Christ. Prior to becoming Christ-followers, we prioritized self-interest above everything else. But as people who have been reconciled to God we no longer look to our own self-interest, but rather, God's glory is the driving motivation behind everything. Paul wrote:

> *I have been crucified with Christ. It is no longer I who live, but Christ who lives in me. And the life I now live in the flesh I live by faith in the Son of God, who loved me and gave himself for me.*
> **GALATIANS 2:20**

How does believing the gospel help us overcome our natural self-interest?

What desires or motivations has Christ helped you crucify?

The miracle at the wedding in Cana revealed change had arrived. The change continues as God transforms men and women through the gospel of Jesus Christ. We are a new people with a new motivation driven by the work of Christ in our lives.

> *Close your time today asking God to help you be an effective ambassador for Christ.*

The Temple, Spiritual Consumerism, and Jesus

GROUP STUDY

Start
Welcome everyone to session 8.

In American culture, when we meet someone for the first time it's common to ask what they do for a living. Why do you think this is a common question in our society?

What types of things do you need to know about someone to feel confident that you know them well?

The last several sessions have taken a close look at John's Gospel and examined passages that reveal insights about Jesus' identity. In this session, continue to take a closer look at who Jesus is and what He does.

How would you describe the difference between what someone does and who they are?

To prepare for video session 8, pray that God will help each person understand and apply this truth:

John reveals what Jesus does in order to show us who Jesus is: a prophet who confronts us, a priest who cleanses us, and a king who constructs the temple of true worship.

Watch

*Use the space below to take notes
while you watch video session 8.*

Discuss

*Use the following questions to guide
your discussion of the video.*

1. Pastor J. T. said that based on John 2:13-22, we see Jesus as "a prophet who challenges the spiritual consumer, He is a priest who cleanses us from sin, and He is a king who builds a temple for God's presence." What do you think He meant by the term "spiritual consumer?"

2. What are the risks of approaching our church life as a spiritual consumer rather than a worshiper?

3. Pastor J. T. said, "The greatest challenge to your faith, day in and day out, is that you would allow spiritual consumerism and your spiritual convenience to distort your view and vision of the glory of Jesus Christ." How is spiritual consumerism a threat to your view of Jesus?

4. How would you describe the holiness of God to a non-believer or new Christian?

5. Why should God's holiness call us to worship with reverence and awe?

6. Name a few ways you see a lack of reverence and disregard for God's holiness within Christian culture.

7. Pastor J. T. said, "Consumer Christianity will tell you Jesus is merciful, but it won't tell you He's holy." Why must we be mindful that Jesus is both merciful and holy?

8. What are some practices we can employ to keep our lives free of spiritual consumerism?

PRAYER REQUESTS

FAMILY DISCIPLESHIP

John reveals what Jesus does to show us who Jesus is: a prophet who confronts us, a priest who cleanses us, and a king who constructs the temple of true worship.

If you need to, reword this week's truth so that your whole family can understand it.

■ **TIME:** Read John 2:13-22. Encourage children to read the Scripture if they're able. Take turns reading the verses out loud. Explain that to know Jesus well, we need to look at different scenes from Jesus' life and ministry. Share that Jesus got angry because people were disrespecting His Father by placing convenience over worship.

■ **MOMENTS:** Throughout the week, encourage children to think about different aspects of Jesus' character. Ask them to describe what they love about Him. Encourage them to verbalize their feelings about Jesus and explain that doing so is an act of worship.

■ **MILESTONES:** Ask children to identify ways they worship God. Point out that worship services, singing, prayer, and Bible study are all ways to worship God. Plan a time of family worship during the week when each family member shares specific attributes of God that move them to worship Him.

CLEANSING THE TEMPLE

Read John 2:13-22.

What did Jesus witness in the temple?

What was Jesus' response to what was going on? Are you comfortable with this aspect of Jesus? Why or why not?

Why did this particular kind of commerce make Jesus so angry?

To celebrate Passover, Jews from surrounding areas traveled to Jerusalem. While there, every participant was required to sacrifice an animal. For those who had traveled a long distance, it was difficult to bring their livestock with them and was much more convenient to purchase their animal to sacrifice once they arrived in Jerusalem. Early on, the commerce booths were set up outside a good distance from the temple. But by Jesus' time, the outer court which was supposed to be a place of prayer and worship for all people had been converted into a place for buying and selling. People had come to worship, but had disrespected God for the sake of convenience.

Where do you think they went wrong in their pursuit of convenience?

A Prophet Who Confronts

Jesus wasn't angry because they we offering a sacrifice or purchasing it once they arrived in Jerusalem. Jesus was angry because they were buying and selling in the temple. He's not challenging the commerce of the day or forbidding convenience. He's challenging the fact that the commerce is happening in the temple. They've traveled all this way to worship and they are missing the point because they are putting themselves at the center of the experience and disrespecting the house of God. The lack of reverence Jesus sees makes Him so angry that He makes a whip of cords, turns over tables, and He drives them out of the temple.

What are some ways we subtly or directly exchange the worship of God for our convenience?

Do you think it's possible for something to begin as well-intentioned but turn into something offensive to God? Can you think of any examples?

What does this passage reveal about how we should worship God?

What responsibility should we take to examine our own practice and discern ways they might be unintentionally dishonoring to God?

Challenging the Status-Quo

His disciples remembered that it was written, "Zeal
for your house will consume me."
JOHN 2:17

Jesus' disciples watched what was taking place and remembered the words David had written centuries before: "For zeal for your house has consumed me, and the reproaches of those who reproach you have fallen on me" (Ps. 69:9). As the disciples watched Jesus clear the temple, they connected His zeal to the zeal David had expressed. The sacred space that had been set apart for worship had become chaotic for the sake of convenience—and Jesus wasn't having it—because it had negatively influenced the people's ability to worship.

What does this account reveal to us about prioritizing worship?

How would you describe your quality of worship at this stage in life? What adjustments might you need to make?

Worship is a crucial aspect in the life of a Christian. To understand who Jesus is, we must recognize that He prioritized worship and had fervent zeal for the house of God above everything else. Worship isn't something we should ignore or approach casually. God's people are called to worship with reverence and intentionality. Like the worshipers at the temple, we should welcome Jesus' challenge to the status quo for the sake of our souls.

Close your time by asking God to help you worship
with reverence and awe. Spend time praising Him
for who He is and the goodness of His nature.

Personal Study 2
A PRIEST WHO CLEANSES

For we do not have a high priest who is unable to sympathize with our weaknesses, but one who in every respect has been tempted as we are, yet without sin.
HEBREWS 4:15

Read the above passage slowly. List every detail it reveals about Jesus.

Why is it important to understand that Jesus sympathized with us in our weakness if we want to have a close relationship with Jesus?

Jesus is a prophet who confronts sin, but He's also a priest who cleanses us from sin. The Bible refers to Jesus as our "High Priest" (Heb. 4:15). In the Old Testament, one of the primary responsibilities of the priest was to cleanse the temple and make sure it was prepared to receive people for worship. But in John 2:13-25, we see the priests had failed to do their job by allowing the temple to become a place of commerce. So Jesus, the true Priest, came in and scourged the temple and He purged it from filthiness and ungodliness.

Why was it loving of Jesus to drive the money-changers out of the temple? What was He trying to teach them?

Can you recall a time when Jesus brought to your attention a sin you didn't realize you were committing? If so, what happened?

Jesus wants to cleanse us from all sin—the ones we are aware of and the ones we don't even know about. The text says "he drove them all out" (2:15). That might sound harsh, but in reality Jesus was demonstrating mercy rather than judgment. It would be judgment if the text said, "He left them there in their sin." Jesus was showing mercy by calling attention to their sins and giving them the opportunity to repent and reprioritize worship above everything else, but some were offended by what He had done.

A King Who Constructs a Temple of Worship

So the Jews said to him, "What sign do you show us for doing these things?" Jesus answered them, "Destroy this temple, and in three days I will raise it up."
JOHN 2:18-19

Why did the Jews question Jesus about what He did in the temple?

What was Jesus referring to when He said, "Destroy this temple and in three days I will raise it up?" How was this later fulfilled?

The Jews were offended by Jesus' actions in the temple because He was exerting authority they wanted to keep for themselves. They asked Jesus for a sign to prove His authority and Jesus refused to give them one (v. 18). Jesus didn't perform miracles on demand for anyone. Instead, He once again referred to His death, burial, and resurrection. The Jews were attempting to domesticate and control Jesus, which is impossible. Spiritual consumers want a sign from Jesus; disciples want Jesus. They demand an immediate sign, but He delays until the resurrection, because God does not operate on our timetable.

What is the difference between wanting a miracle from Jesus and wanting Jesus?

We often think we want a god we can control but why would a god who we could control not be God at all?

How does Jesus offer something far better than spiritual consumerism?

What we've seen unfold in the temple is a conflict between spiritual consumerism and true worship, and the only answer to spiritual consumerism is a better view of Jesus. Jesus reveals Himself as a prophet, a priest, and a king. As true worshipers of God, we will be more enthralled with who Jesus is than what He does. As Christians, we have the privilege of knowing Jesus—not just what He does for us—but who He is. There is no higher honor.

> *Close your time today by thanking God that Jesus reveals Himself as a prophet, priest, and king. Tell Him you want to worship Him for who He is and savor His lordship.*

An Inadequate Faith

GROUP STUDY

Start

Welcome everyone to session 9.

Who is your favorite actor, singer, or athlete? What do you like about them?

With so much media and technology at our fingertips, we can learn more about people than ever. If you're a fan of a specific artist or celebrity, there's a good chance you know about their work, what city they live in, and even details about their personal life. But knowing factual information about someone is very different than having a relationship.

Who are the people who know you the best? Are you easy to get to know? Why or why not?

It might be silly to think we know our favorite celebrity when we've never met them, but it would be tragic only to know factual information about Jesus and mistakenly believe we truly know Him.

To prepare for video session 9, pray that God will help each person understand and apply this truth:

The Gospel of John encourages us to examine our relationships with Jesus and ensure that we know Him personally rather than simply knowing information about Him.

Watch

*Use the space below to take notes
while you watch video session 9.*

Discuss

*Use the following questions to guide
your discussion of the video.*

1. Pastor Matt said, "When the church focuses all its energy on felt needs rather than the gospel of Jesus Christ, she gets thin and weak and her joy is sapped because she's trying to use God, not love Him. We're trying to use God to get what we actually want, not worshiping Jesus for who He is." What is the difference between loving God and attempting to use Him to get what you want?

2. What are the differences between felt needs and ultimate needs. How would you describe the difference between the two?

3. How do we know if we've made a false need an ultimate need? Why do "felt needs" make lousy gods?

4. In this week's passage, the people loved the signs (miracles) Jesus was doing, but they didn't love Jesus. How is this possibility a threat to the modern-day church? If so, what examples can you think of?

5. We all want to be blessed by God. How can you tell if you truly love Jesus apart from His blessings?

6. Have you ever experienced a time when it felt like Jesus was withholding something from you for a period of time? How did you respond? What did you learn through that process?

7. Pastor Matt defined faith as "the turning to Christ for our justification and away from ourselves." How would you explain this to someone exploring Christianity?

8. Pastor Matt said, "The good news of the gospel of Jesus Christ is not that if you give your life to Jesus everything goes the way you want it. It's that regardless of what comes, Jesus will be there and you will find Him to be enough." How have you found this to be true in your own life?

PRAYER REQUESTS

FAMILY DISCIPLESHIP

The Gospel of John encourages us to examine our relationships with Jesus and ensure that we know Him personally rather than simply knowing information about Him.

If you need to reword this week's truth so that your whole family can understand it.

■ **TIME:** Read John 2:23-25. Encourage children to read the Scripture if they're able. Take turns reading the verses out loud. Explain that some people loved the miracles that Jesus did and the things He provided for them but they didn't really love Jesus.

■ **MOMENTS:** Throughout the week, encourage children to think about different aspects of Jesus' character and personality. Ask them to describe what they enjoy most about Him. Explain that it's natural to love the way Jesus provides for us. But share that our love for Jesus is to be based on who He is rather than what He provides.

■ **MILESTONES:** Celebrate specific spiritual markers that relate to faith. Examples might include becoming a believer, being baptized, or anything that played a significant role in your child's spiritual development.

Personal Study 1

TRUE FAITH

Now when he was in Jerusalem at the Passover Feast, many believed in his name when they saw the signs that he was doing. But Jesus on his part did not entrust himself to them, because he knew all people and needed no one to bear witness about man, for he himself knew what was in man.
JOHN 2:23-25

What led the crowds to "believe" in Jesus? How would you describe their faith?

How did Jesus respond to their "belief"? What does His response teach us about His identity?

Unlike the rest of us, Jesus cannot be tricked by flattery or lured by praise. He knows what's in people's hearts and He understood that the people referred to in the above passage were enthralled with His performance rather than His identity as the Son of God. They weren't interested in who He was but what He could do for them. As a result, Jesus didn't "entrust Himself" to them (v. 24) meaning Jesus withheld revealing Himself to them because of their shallow and inauthentic faith.

How would you describe the difference between a general faith in God's existence compared to saving faith that demands you follow Jesus as Lord?

How do we confuse the two?

Many people know facts about Jesus without having a relationship with Him. These people have no intention of ever following Him. They just know some facts about Him. True believers love and trust Jesus in every area of their lives. True belief produces fruit.

What characteristics accompany someone who loves and trusts Jesus?

When did your own faith change from knowing about Jesus to truly following Jesus?

Evidence of Saving Faith

Many claim the Christian faith but far fewer live as authentic followers of Jesus. To be sure, we all sin and fall short of the glory of God even after we become believers (Rom. 3:23). Even people who love Jesus above all things have days (or weeks) when they completely miss the mark. But the Bible teaches that people who love and trust Jesus live in a way that makes them distinct. Jesus said:

> *"If you love me, you will keep my commandments."*
> **JOHN 14:15**

How does obedience to Jesus make a Christian distinct from the world around them?

What might it mean if someone claims to love Jesus, but habitually lives a lifestyle that disregards His Word?

What new insight does this passage give to change the way we think of obedience?

Jesus made it clear: If we love Him, we will obey Him—not because we are forced to—but because we want to. When we truly love God, our desires start to align with His will for our lives. We begin to want the same things He wants and have a desire to live a life that brings Him glory. It doesn't mean we will be perfect—far from it. Jesus is the only One who is without sin. But if we love Jesus, we will experience a desire to obey His Word and will feel conviction when we disobey Him. The author of Psalm 119 wrote:

> *Teach me, O LORD, the way of your statutes;*
> *and I will keep it to the end.*
> *Give me understanding, that I may keep your law*
> *and observe it with my whole heart.*
> *Lead me in the path of your commandments,*
> *for I delight in it.*
> **PSALM 119:33-35**

These words by the psalmist were not written by a man who considered God's commands to be burdensome. On the contrary, he delighted in it (v. 35). Jesus and His Word are so interconnected that we can't love one and disregard the other. If we love Jesus, we will obey His Word.

> *Close your time asking God to give you a heart that loves Him above all things. Ask Him to increase your desire for Him and to give you a delight for the Scriptures.*

Personal Study 2
COUNTERFEIT OR AUTHENTIC?

As seen in the previous personal study, there is a kind of belief that Jesus doesn't recognize as saving faith. When we love and trust Jesus, we obey Him (John 14:15). Today, we'll look at additional passages that reveal what saving faith looks like. In Matthew's Gospel, Jesus differentiated between counterfeit and authentic faith.

> *Beware of false prophets, who come to you in sheep's clothing but inwardly are ravenous wolves. You will recognize them by their fruits. Are grapes gathered from thornbushes, or figs from thistles? So, every healthy tree bears good fruit, but the diseased tree bears bad fruit. A healthy tree cannot bear bad fruit, nor can a diseased tree bear good fruit.*
> **MATTHEW 7:15-18**

What analogies did Jesus use to explain the difference between genuine believers and false prophets?

How do these metaphors help us identify false teachers among us?

How would you describe the difference between good fruit and bad fruit?

Jesus taught that God's people will be confronted with false prophets who present themselves to be godly, but in reality, they are dangerous predators intent to do harm. Jesus said we could tell if they are genuine or not by how they behave. Certainly, it's wise to listen to what people have to say. But if what someone says isn't backed up by the way they live, something is wrong. Authentic faith is represented by consistency between words and actions.

How can you tell the difference between someone who makes a mistake and someone who consistently bears bad fruit?

Why is it sometimes difficult to admit someone is not who you thought them to be?

Why is it loving or even helpful to identify false prophets?

Loving God Means Loving People

Saving faith in Jesus Christ influences how we live. If someone claims to be a Christian yet no evidence of that manifests itself in their character over a long period of time, there is reason for concern. We need to keep in mind that people don't start in the same place and therefore we can't expect people to reach spiritual maturity at the same rate. However, we can expect there to be signs of change. Jesus taught there are specific indicators that accompany genuine faith. Just before going to the cross, Jesus told His disciples how the world would know we belong to Him:

A new commandment I give to you, that you love one another: just as I have loved you, you also are to love one another. By this all people will know that you are my disciples, if you have love for one another.
JOHN 13:34-35

What does it mean to love others the way Jesus has loved us?

Do you think most Christians are known for their love for each other? Why or why not?

Practically speaking, what would it look like for believers to be known for their love?

Who in your local church can you demonstrate the love of Christ to this week?

Jesus didn't say the world would recognize a Christ-follower by his politics, profession, material possessions, or social status. He said the world would recognize we belonged to Him if we loved each other in the same way He has loved us. Evidence of saving faith reveals itself in love for God, obedience to His Word, and love for one another (John 13:34-35; 14:15). If you want to know if someone truly loves Jesus, take a look at their life and their love..

> *Close your time in prayer by asking God to deepen your love for Him and for other people. Give thanks for the gift of saving faith.*

Born of the Spirit

GROUP STUDY

Start

Welcome everyone to session 10.

List the variety of ways people relate to you. Examples might include son/daughter, brother/sister, and so on.

How do your relationships differ depending on the context? For instance, how might your relationship with your parents be different than with a sibling?

All of us fill roles in other people's lives. We are sons and daughters, brothers and sisters, moms and dads, employers and employees, friends and neighbors. Our relationships contain similarities, but they also have differences depending on the context. In this session, we'll be introduced to a man named Nicodemus. Nicodemus approached Jesus as a rabbi and great teacher, and Jesus was a Rabbi and a great teacher. However, we'll see why Jesus fills a far more significant role than those titles.

What are some of the ways you relate to Jesus?

To prepare for video session 10, pray that God will help each person understand and apply this truth:

Those who are born of the Spirit practice repentance by turning away from sin and turning toward Christ.

Watch

Use the space below to take notes while you watch video session 10.

Video sessions available at lifeway.com/johnbiblestudy

Discuss

*Use the following questions to guide
your discussion of the video.*

1. What roles does Jesus fill in your life? Why is Jesus able to fill numerous roles while people are only able to fill one or two? (i.e. having a spouse who is also your friend).

2. Nicodemus approached Jesus as a rabbi and teacher. Why was this an accurate assessment? What was Nicodemus missing about Jesus?

3. John 3:1-8 teaches that we are not only to relate to Jesus in the flesh but we must be "born again" and relate to Him in the Spirit. Why is the concept of being "born again" difficult for some people to accept?

4. To be born again we must repent. Pastor Matt defined repentance as "turning from sin to know, love, trust, and obey Jesus." Why does repentance have to be a lifestyle rather than a one-time event?

5. Why is belief and faith, like repentance, a continuous act that must be chosen over and over? What does this look like practically?

6. Pastor Matt said, "For the rest of our lives, you and I, to relate rightly to God, are going to turn away from sin and toward knowing, loving, and obeying Jesus. We're going to stumble and fall. We're going to fall short. We're going to mess up. We're going to not do what we're supposed to do. We have to keep repenting and keep turning back." How does this daily practice bring the grace and mercy of God to bear on our lives?

7. Why do we tend to delay repentance? What effect does this have on our lives?

8. Pastor Matt described evidence of the Holy Spirit's work as "the wind blowing." What evidence of "the wind blowing" have you seen recently in your own life?

PRAYER REQUESTS

FAMILY DISCIPLESHIP

Those who are born of the Spirit practice repentance by turning away from sin and turning toward Christ.

If you need to, reword this week's truth so that your whole family can understand it.

■ **TIME:** Read John 3:1-8. Encourage children to read the Scripture if they're able. Take turns reading the verses out loud. Draw attention to Jesus' conversation with Nicodemus and point out that Nicodemus related to Jesus as a great teacher. Explain that Jesus was a great teacher but that He was more than a teacher. Share that Jesus is our Savior, and we are to turn away from our sin (repent) and turn to Jesus.

■ **MOMENTS:** Ask children to identify different ways they relate to Jesus. Examples might include Savior, Teacher, Friend, Healer, or Helper. Explain that because Jesus is God, He has the ability to fill numerous roles and meet all of our needs.

■ **MILESTONES:** Encourage children to reminisce and celebrate ways Jesus has been faithful to meet their needs. Recall times they got through a challenging time at school, recovered from an illness, or overcame a specific fear with the help of Jesus.

Personal Study 1

A MAN NAMED NICODEMUS

Read John 3:1-8.

What was Nicodemus' standing among the Jews? Why does this matter?

What seems to have led Nicodemus to visit Jesus? Why did he come at night?

Nicodemus was a man in high standing among the leaders of Israel and would have been considered a member of the religious elite. He was also a theologian and a "teacher of Israel" (v. 10). Nicodemus was a man who had likely spent a lot of time studying the Old Testament Scriptures, and yet he didn't understand what Jesus was teaching him, and he didn't recognize Jesus as the Messiah. Jesus was causing a lot of talk among the Pharisees, so it's not surprising Nicodemus chose to visit Jesus. Because Nicodemus visited Jesus at night, it's possible he didn't want people to know, or perhaps he wanted to question Jesus privately.

Nicodemus said "Rabbi, we know that you are a teacher come from God..." (v. 2). Do you think that Nicodemus was speaking for himself or the religious group he represented?

What other elements of Jesus' identity was Nicodemus missing?

How did who Nicodemus believed Jesus to be shape the way he approached and related to Jesus?

How do our own assumptions and understanding of Jesus impact the way to relate to Him?

You Must Be Born-Again

The religious rulers of the Jews had concerns about Jesus. He had been the topic of much discussion, but Nicodemus' words were diplomatic. He even went as far as to acknowledge that Jesus was a gifted teacher of God (v. 2). But Jesus didn't even acknowledge Nicodemus' statement. Instead, Jesus got straight to the point. Jesus answered him, "Truly, truly, I say to you, unless one is born again he cannot see the kingdom of God" (John 3:3).

What comes to mind when you hear the term "born-again?"

How would you describe the term to a non-believer?

Why did Jesus redirect Nicodemus so quickly?

Water and Spirit

Jesus wasn't interested in Nicodemus' flattering statement. Remember, Jesus knows what's in the heart of all people (John 2:25). Jesus knew Nicodemus lacked saving faith, and so Jesus explained that in addition to our natural birth, people must experience a spiritual rebirth to become children of God and members of His kingdom. Nicodemus didn't understand what Jesus was saying and told Him as much (v. 4). But Jesus didn't falter or backdown. To be born of water and the Spirit means we have been spiritually transformed and given inward renewal that can only come from God's work in our lives.

Why do people resist the concept of spiritual rebirth or being born-again?

In verse 8, Jesus compares the Holy Spirit to the "wind." Why is this a fitting analogy? What role does the Holy Spirit play in being born-again?

To be a Christian, Jesus says we must be born-again through the Holy Spirit. To be born of God means we must be born of the Spirit. Jesus compares the wind to the spirit. The wind is invisible, but you can see the effects of the wind. In the same way, the Spirit is invisible but the effects are obvious. All believers have the Holy Spirit (Gal. 4:6). He is the agent that brings transformation and renewal.

> *Close your time in prayer by giving thanks to God for the gift of spiritual rebirth and the forgiveness of sins.*

Personal Study 2
LIFE IN THE SPIRIT

For all who are led by the Spirit of God are sons of God.
ROMANS 8:14

In the previous personal study, we mentioned that the Holy Spirit was like a blowing wind. What does that look like? If you open up the Bible at your house and read it, when we gather here in the name of Jesus, when you choose right over wrong because you love Jesus, these are all examples of the wind blowing.

When are you most mindful of the Spirit's work in your life?

List some of the specific ways you've recently seen "the wind blowing."

All God's children are led by the Spirit of God. How would you describe that truth in your own words? Practically speaking, what does that look like?

The Role of the Holy Spirit

Look up the following passages and write down what these Scriptures reveal about the Holy Spirit.

John 16:8-11

John 16:12-15

Romans 8:14

Romans 8:16

Romans 8:26

Acts 20:22

Acts 20:23

What new insights did you learn from these passages?

The Holy Spirit remains a mystery to many believers, and because we are so unfamiliar with His roles we miss Him and fail to see evidence of His work in our lives. But when we are born-again and become children of God, the Holy Spirit becomes an integral part of our lives. The Holy Spirit has been given to us to help us in the practical matters of day-to-day living. Jesus knew we would need a Helper, and He gave us one (John 14:26).

In what ways have you been guilty of ignoring the Holy Spirit's presence in your life?

After reading the Scripture passages, can you identify things the Holy Spirit has done in your life where you haven't given Him adequate credit?

A Helper

Jesus offered a simple description of the Holy Spirit—a Helper:

> *Nevertheless, I tell you the truth: it is to your advantage*
> *that I go away, for if I do not go away, the Helper will*
> *not come to you. But if I go, I will send him to you.*
> **JOHN 16:7**

Why would Jesus leaving be to the disciples' advantage?

How is the Holy Spirit a Helper?

What outcome or situations can you attribute to the power of the Holy Spirit in your life today?

Just before going to the cross, Jesus gathered His disciples, and one of the things He told them to anticipate was the Holy Spirit. Jesus understood that we needed the power of God to live the Christian life because we can't do it on our own. If we didn't need help, there would've been no need to send a Helper—but He did. The Christian life is not simply difficult—it is impossible apart from the Holy Spirit. And God doesn't expect us to attempt it apart from the power of the Spirit.

> *Close your time in prayer giving thanks to God*
> *for giving the gift of the Holy Spirit.*

A Love That Gives and Sends

GROUP STUDY

Start

Welcome everyone to session 11.

Do you think of love most often as a noun or a verb?

People are enthralled with the concept of love. In every generation, love has been the topic of countless books, songs, and movies. People can't get enough of it. Interestingly, the concept of love is the focus of the most well-known passage in the New Testament: "For God so loved the world, that he gave his only Son, that whoever believes in him should not perish but have eternal life (John 3:16).

How does our culture and the media depict love? Do you think it's an accurate assessment? Why or why not?

What do you know about love now that you'd wish you'd known earlier.

To prepare for video session 11, pray that God will help each person understand and apply this truth:

> Jesus' mission to seek and save sinners reveals the love of God that gives and sends freely and fully.

Watch

*Use the space below to take notes
while you watch video session 11.*

Video sessions available at lifeway.com/johnbiblestudy

Discuss

*Use the following questions to guide
your discussion of the video.*

1. Nicodemus wrongly believed his religious credentials were enough to get him into heaven. What are some ways we unwittingly believe our religious credentials are enough to get us into heaven? Why is this not true?

2. During Jesus' conversation with Nicodemus He referred to an Old Testament story from the Book of Numbers. Why do you think Jesus appealed to Nicodemus' knowledge of the Old Testament?

3. Pastor Trevor said, "Jesus is trying to point out to Nicodemus our radical corruption from sin requires a radical redemption from God. As Jesus has been saying to Nicodemus, we need a brand new birth." Why is it impossible for us to see our need for redemption if we don't understand the magnitude of our sin problem?

4. The words "trust and believe" are used 241 times throughout the New Testament, 98 times just within the Gospel of John. Why do you think it is a theme we see over and over?

5. Practically speaking, what does it look like to "trust and believe" in our daily life?

6. Pastor Trevor explained that God's love is one that "gives and sends." Why must we "receive" from God before we can "give" to others?

7. If you are a believer, what might it look like for you to "be sent" to share the gospel with other people?

8. Who were the people who were instrumental in telling you about Jesus and teaching you what it means to be a Christian? How could you model that same service to other people?

PRAYER REQUESTS

FAMILY DISCIPLESHIP

Jesus' mission to seek and save sinners reveals the love of God that gives and sends freely and fully.

If you need to, reword this week's truth so that your whole family can understand it.

■ **TIME:** Read John 3:9-21. Encourage children to read the Scripture if they're able. Take turns reading the verses out loud. Draw attention to John 3:16. Explain that God's love is deep and that He sent His Son so we could spend eternity with Him.

■ **MOMENTS:** Ask children to put John 3:16 in their own words. Explain that God's love for us motivated Him to send Jesus—God's sinless Son—to save us from our sins. Talk about the fact that love is sacrificial and that love requires that we make sacrifices too. Share that because God has given freely to us, we are to give freely and fully to others.

■ **MILESTONES:** Encourage children to talk about what led up to them becoming a Christian. Reach out to pastors, Sunday school teachers, or friends who were instrumental in sharing the gospel. Consider writing a note to thank them.

HOW CAN THESE THINGS BE?

In the last session, we spent time discussing a conversation between Jesus and Nicodemus when Jesus shared some hard truths. Nicodemus was a religious man—a Pharisee, and member of the Sanhedrin. By that day's standards, Nicodemus was considered a member of the religious elite. But Jesus told Nicodemus that religious credentials aren't enough to get anyone into the kingdom of God—we must be born again (John 3:3). Today, we'll pick up midway through the conversation.

Read John 3:9-15.

Nicodemus lacked understanding and asked, "How can these things be?" Jesus rebuked him but also had compassion and took time to explain things. What does this reveal to us about the heart of Christ?

When have you experienced God's compassion when you didn't understand?

Merciful Judgment

Nicodemus didn't understand what Jesus was saying so Jesus directed their conversation to a story about the Israelites found in the Book of Numbers. God had delivered the people from slavery in Egypt, and provided for their needs, but as they traveled back to Canaan, the people complained and were impatient with God and Moses. Their attitude and behavior demonstrated rebellion and God responded in judgment by sending a plaque of poisonous snakes (Num. 21:4-6).

God's judgment had it's intended effect—the people repented of their wicked behavior. When God saw that the people had repented, He responded in mercy. "And the LORD said to Moses, 'Make a fiery serpent and set it on a pole, and everyone who is bitten, when he sees it, shall live.'" (Num. 21:8).

How was God's act of judgment ultimately an act of mercy?

Why does it sometimes take difficult circumstances to motivate us to repent?

What is Jesus' point in telling this story about the bronze serpent to Nicodemus?

What did Jesus mean when He said, "so must the Son of Man be lifted up"? (v. 14).

The Son of Man Must Be Lifted Up

Jesus recalled this story to Nicodemus to make a comparison. When Jesus used the phrase, "lifted up" He was speaking to the fact that He would be lifted up on a cross. For people to become children of God, and to enter His kingdom, He would have to take on the sting of death and suffer the horrors of the cross.

Glance back to John 3:15. What would be the outcome for those who believe in the Son of Man?

What would be the outcome for those who failed to believe?

Why is it so easy for us, like Nicodemus, to confuse religious performance of biblical knowledge for saving faith?

John wrote in his first epistle, "Whoever has the Son has life; whoever does not have the Son of God does not have life" (1 John 5:12). How do these truths prove that there is not multiple paths to God?

Jesus explained that He would be "lifted up" on a cross so that "whoever believes in him may have eternal life" (3:15). Jesus' point parallels the Israelites in the wilderness. Those who had suffered from snakebites were going to die, but God gave them a remedy to prevent their destruction (21:8). In Jesus' teaching to Nicodemus, He revealed that because of sin, all of humankind is in a state of deadly spiritual peril. Our only cure for sin is to look to Jesus and His work on the cross. Only in looking to Jesus can we be saved from our sin.

*Close your time in prayer, giving thanks to God for providing
a remedy in Jesus Christ for our fatal spiritual condition.*

Personal Study 2
FOR GOD SO LOVED THE WORLD

Read John 3:16-21.

Without a doubt, John 3:16 is the most well-known passages in the New Testament. It's seen on T-shirts, bumper stickers, and written on signs in the stands at professional sporting events. Sadly, it's also a passage that is frequently taken out of context.

> *For God so loved the world, that he gave his only Son, that whoever believes in him should not perish but have eternal life.*
> **JOHN 3:16**

Restate John 3:16 is the simplest form:

Some people read John 3:16 and come to the false conclusion that God offers universal salvation regardless of what someone believes or who they worship. They believe all paths lead to God. In our culture, some would assert that if God was really loving He would have provided a variety of options. But God didn't provide a variety of options—He provided One. The text says that God's love is so deep that He sent His only Son. True belief is conditioned upon belief in the Son.

Why do you think people get angry when they hear there is only one way to God?

Considering the problem human beings have always had with sin, we should be shocked God provided any path to eternal life. How does the sense of injustice some feel when they learn Jesus is the only way reveal a lack of understanding about our sin nature?

For God did not send his Son into the world to condemn the world, but in order that the world might be saved through him. Whoever believes in him is not condemned, but whoever does not believe is condemned already, because he has not believed in the name of the only Son of God.
JOHN 3:17-18

What was God's reason for sending His Son?

Those who believe in Jesus aren't condemned. What is the alternative for those who don't believe? Why should this lead us to tell others about Jesus with urgency?

Jesus' mission in coming to this world was to save people. Those who believe in Christ and trust His work on the cross for their salvation will not be condemned. But those who refuse Christ are condemned because there is no other option for being reconciled to God. Apart from Jesus, we live in darkness. John wrote, "And this is the judgment: the light has come into the world, and people loved the darkness rather than the light because their works were evil" (John 3:19).

No Other Name

And there is salvation in no one else, for there is no other name under heaven given among men by which we must be saved.
ACTS 4:12

Why is the lie of "there are many ways to heaven" so prevalent?

In John 14:6 Jesus said, "I am the way, and the truth, and the life. No one comes to the Father except through me." What is your response to the reality that there is only one way?

Who do you need to share the saving plan of God with this week?

God didn't send His sinless Son to die on a cruel Roman cross so He could be one among many paths to salvation. Jesus is the only path. God's motivation was love: it's a love given to us that sends us into the world to tell our friends and neighbors about the only love that saves. When we freely receive the gift of salvation, it is our responsibility to share it with others.

> *Close your time in prayer giving thanks to God that there is no condemnation for those who believe in Christ. Ask Him to lead you to people who need to hear the good news of the gospel.*

SESSION 12

Our Place and Message

GROUP STUDY

Start
Welcome everyone to session 12.

Think about a couple of your favorite restaurants or stores. What are specific ways they compete with one another?

What types of things motivate you to recommend a place of business to a friend?

We live in a consumer-driven culture where customer satisfaction is paramount. If a company doesn't meet our needs, we take our business elsewhere. In a consumer-driven society, it's natural and even appropriate for business owners to compete. But a competitor's mindset has no place in the church. If we belong to Jesus, it's our calling to work together for the kingdom of God. Our job is to collectively point as many people to Jesus as possible.

What would it look like for churches to work together to serve the kingdom of God?

> *To prepare for video session 12, pray that God will help each person understand and apply this truth:*

> We pursue gospel-centered multiplication to point as many people as possible to Jesus.

Watch

Use the space below to take notes
while you watch video session 12.

.

Video sessions available at lifeway.com/johnbiblestudy

Discuss

*Use the following questions to guide
your discussion of the video.*

1. In the video teaching, Pastor Matt's two points were that "we need to know our place and our message." How would you describe your place and your message?

2. How would you describe the difference between an allegiance to Jesus versus an allegiance to your own desires and preferences for church?

3. Pastor Matt said "Our place is to be happy under the sovereign reign of God." How does being happy serving God reduce our desire for infighting and competition?

4. Pastor Matt said, "What happens all too often is local churches believe they are the only ones in town who have found the right mixture of open-hand and closed-hand theology and has woven it together in such a way that's better than all other churches." Why will this mindset inevitably bring a poor outcome?

5. Why is it inappropriate when churches and ministries compete with each other? What is the godly response when we see another church or ministry succeed?

6. What is our role in helping other churches and ministries succeed?

7. If we truly believe Jesus above all and over all, how will it be obvious in the ways we relate to other churches and ministries?

8. What might change if God's people reached out to other churches and across denominational lines with the goal of telling more people about Jesus?

9. What obstacles prevent us from serving alongside other churches, or even other believers?

PRAYER REQUESTS

FAMILY DISCIPLESHIP

If you need to, reword this week's truth so that
your whole family can understand it.

We pursue gospel-centered multiplication to
point as many people as possible to Jesus.

■ **TIME:** Read John 3:22-36. Encourage children to read the Scripture if they're able. Take turns reading the verses out loud. Point out that John the Baptist's disciples were uneasy because people were going to Jesus to be baptized. Explain that John the Baptist taught that we are to work together to point as many people to Jesus as possible.

■ **MOMENTS:** When you are out and about in your community, point out numerous churches and ministries who are working to point people to Jesus. Ask your children where their friends worship. Encourage them to be familiar with places outside your local church who are actively engaging in gospel-centered ministry.

■ **MILESTONES:** Plan a special day when your family serves alongside another local church or ministry in your community. Examples might include another church congregation, homeless shelter, soup kitchen, or church plant.

JESUS ABOVE ALL

In this final session of study, we'll look at a conversation between John the Baptist and his disciples. We'll see that when we know our place and message that we experience great joy when the kingdom of God advances.

Read John 3:22-36.

Why were John the Baptist's disciples concerned about Jesus' ministry (v. 26)?

In what areas are you prone to envy? How do you act when you feel envious?

Were John's disciples concerns natural or selfish? Explain why you feel the way you do.

I Am Not the Christ

John the Baptist and his disciples were baptizing people in the Judean country-side when John's disciples noticed that more and more people were going to Jesus to be baptized rather than John (v. 26). Andrew, Peter's brother, had already left John to follow Jesus (1:35-41), but John still had a group of disciples who con-tinued to travel with him. These men were loyal to John and felt threatened when they realized their ministry was losing momentum. The situation bothered them so much they brought it to John's attention. John responded in a noteworthy manner:

You yourselves bear me witness, that I said, 'I am not the Christ,
but I have been sent before him.' The one who has the bride is the
bridegroom. The friend of the bridegroom, who stands and hears
him, rejoices greatly at the bridegroom's voice. Therefore this joy
of mine is now complete. He must increase, but I must decrease.
JOHN 3:28-30

What stands out about John's response?

Why did John welcome the success of Jesus' ministry?

John said, "He must increase, but I must decrease." Why is this statement true for everyone who follows Jesus?

Joy That Is Complete

From the beginning, John the Baptist had identified himself as "the voice of one crying in the wilderness" (Matt. 3:3) who would prepare people for the coming of the Lord. John was sent as the forerunner to Jesus so he gladly embraced Christ's arrival. John had been pointing people to Jesus and his ministry was bearing fruit. To explain, John used the analogy of the bridegroom and the best man (3:29). John pointed out that the bride (the church) didn't belong to him—it belonged to Jesus. But John felt great joy in seeing things unfold and said, "Therefore this joy of mine is now complete" (3:29b).

Why could John experience joy even as his ministry was winding down?

How does this passage reveal that John the Baptist understood his place in the kingdom?

Even as John's ministry began to wind down, do you think he had been faithful to his calling? Why or why not?

When we live with the mindset that "Jesus is above all," how can we be content and even happy when another person, church, or ministry experiences a win for the kingdom of God?

The best antidote to envy or spiritual hoarding of resources (time, people, money) and envy is to be captivated by the sovereignty of God and to view success and failure, placement and calling all under the guise of a good God's sovereign plan. John the Baptist understood his role as a forerunnner who would prepare people for Jesus' coming. Knowing his place freed John to rejoice in the Father's sovereign plan. When we acknowledge Jesus above all, we will have complete joy when we see His kingdom advancing.

Close your time in prayer by asking God to show you your place in ministry. Give thanks that in His sovereign plan He enlists His people to build His kingdom.

Personal Study 2

HE MUST INCREASE

He must increase, but I must decrease.
JOHN 3:30

In the previous personal study, we discussed a conversation between John and his disciples who were concerned that Jesus' ministry was surpassing John's. In this conversation, John spoke the most well-known words to ever be uttered from his mouth: "He must increase, but I must decrease" (3:30). John's calling was to go before Jesus and announce His coming, and then fade into the background as Jesus emerged as the Son of God and long-awaited Messiah.

Read John 3:31-36.

According to John, what was Jesus' status (v. 31)?

How did John's view of Jesus "above all" inform his life and ministry?

John made a series of statements about Jesus. In your own words, how would you summarize what he said?

His Place and His Message

John the Baptist understood his place and his message because he had come to terms with Christ's identity. He said, "He who comes from above is above all" (John 3:31a). Only when we get that right can everything else fall in correct order. John knew Jesus had come from the Father and had come to Earth with a message and was declaring the very words of God.

Think about your own life for a moment. Do you live with an awareness that Jesus is above all? Why or why not?

What would it look like for you to reorganize your life in a way that demonstrates that Jesus is above all?

In a few phrases, how would you summarize your place and your message?

The Spirit Without Measure

*For he whom God has sent utters the words of
God, for he gives the Spirit without measure.*
JOHN 3:34

In our quest to live lives that exalt Jesus above all, these words should encourage us. God doesn't give the Spirit in partial measure but in immeasurable dimensions. This is beautiful news for those of us who feel stagnant, confused, trapped in cycles of addiction, or in broken ways of thinking. We don't have to be stuck within the boundaries of our broken limitations—we get the Spirit without measure. The

Spirit empowers us to live spiritually vibrant lives that bring glory to God and do things we could never accomplish in our own strength. When we rely on the Holy Spirit to strengthen and empower us we have the ability to obey God, fulfill our callings, and live a life we could never bring to pass in our own effort.

In what specific areas do you need to rely on the Holy Spirit's power to enable you to do what you can't do in your own strength?

On a scale of 1 to 10, how mindful are you that the Holy Spirit is an ever-present help and that God gives the Spirit without measure?

Think for a moment about the new things you've learned during the last 12 sessions. What stands out to you?

As our study comes to a close, let's remind ourselves of John's reason for writing the Gospel that bears his name. "Now Jesus did many other signs in the presence of the disciples, which are not written in this book; but these are written so that you may believe that Jesus is the Christ, the Son of God, and that by believing you may have life in his name" (John 20:30-31). As we conclude our study, let's remain mindful that the starting point in the Christian life is believing that Jesus is the Son of God—but it doesn't stop there. The Christian life is a life of believing—and having life in His name.

Give thanks to God for the new insights you've learned from the study of John's Gospel. Ask Him to give you the Spirit without measure. Pray He will equip you to live with the mindset that Jesus is above all.

John 1-3
LEADER GUIDE

1. PRAYERFULLY PREPARE

Prepare for each group session with prayer. Ask the Holy Spirit to work through you and the group discussion as you point to Jesus each week through God's Word.

2. ENCOURAGE DISCUSSION

A good small-group experience has the following characteristics.

EVERYONE PARTICIPATES. Encourage everyone to ask questions, share responses, or read aloud.

NO ONE DOMINATES—NOT EVEN THE LEADER. Be sure your time speaking as a leader takes up less than half your time together as a group. Politely guide discussion if anyone dominates.

DON'T RUSH THROUGH QUESTIONS. Don't feel that a moment of silence is a bad thing. People often need time to think about their responses to questions they've just heard or to gain courage to share what God is stirring in their hearts.

AFFIRM AND FOLLOW UP ON INPUT. Make sure you point out something true or helpful in a response. Don't just move on. Build community with follow-up questions, asking how other people have experienced similar things or how a truth has shaped their understanding of God and the Scripture you're studying.

KEEP GOD AND HIS WORD CENTRAL. Opinions and experiences can be helpful, but God has given us the truth. Trust Scripture to be the authority and God's Spirit to work in people's lives. You can't change anyone, but God can. Continually point people to the Word and to active steps of faith.

3. KEEP CONNECTING

Think of ways to connect with group members during the week. Participation during the group session always improves when members spend time connecting with one another outside the group sessions. The more people are comfortable with one another and involved in one another's lives, the more they'll look forward to being together.

Encourage group members with thoughts, commitments, or questions from the session by connecting through emails, texts, and social media. Build deeper friendships by planning or spontaneously inviting group members to join you outside your regularly scheduled group time for meals, fun activities, and projects around your home, church, or community.

4. LEAD GROUP SESSIONS

Thank you for being willing to lead a group through an in-depth examination of the John 1-3. If this is your first time leading a group, don't overthink it. Prepare to lead by viewing the video session, reading the suggestions for the group session, and completing the personal study each week. Be prepared to distribute Bible-study books and to show each video session. For session 1 you'll want to familiarize group members with the format of the study, including the way the group session will be structured ("Start," "Watch," "Discuss") and the features of the Bible-study book ("Family Discipleship" and two personal studies each week). In addition, use the following guides to help you prepare for the group sessions.

Group Session 1

Session 1 introduces the study of John's Gospel. John wrote His Gospel so people would believe that Jesus is the Son of God and by believing they would find life in His name (John 20:31). John opens his prologue by immediately revealing Jesus' identity. Spend time discussing why knowing what you believe about Jesus' identity is foundational to the Christian faith.

Explain that each time the group meets, you'll start the session by reviewing the previous week's topic. Your review will follow the outline of the video session and homework. Emphasize the importance of engaging with the Scriptures throughout the week.

NOTES

....

....

....

Group Session 2

Beginning this week, you'll start each group session by reviewing the previous week's study. This is an important time of sharing, encouragement, and accountability. Evaluate the time you've allotted for the session and aim to manage that time well, allowing time to start with the review and to discuss the teaching after the video.

This session focuses on the topic of God-given belief. The primary goal of this lesson should be to discuss how God initiates and sustains our faith. Encourage group members to share personal studies as they relate to the study, but be sure your time together is focused on the Scriptures.

NOTES

....

....

....

....

Group Session 3

At this point group members should start getting comfortable with the format. This week focuses on the topic of God's grace. Emphasize how this ties in with last week's lesson on God-given belief. God gives us the faith to believe and that is the starting point of the Christian life. In Christ, we have all been given "grace upon grace." Encourage group members to identify specific ways God has given them grace and have them talk about ways they are relying on future grace.

NOTES

....

....

....

....

Group Session 4

John the Baptist was a man who knew who he was and what he was called to do. Notably, John also knew who he wasn't. If we want to follow Jesus, John is someone who we can look to and learn from. Spend time discussing how we can only know who we are by understanding our identity in Jesus. Encourage group members to discuss what it means to say, like John the Baptist, "I am not the Christ." Emphasize the reality that this is a lifelong process and because of our nature something we will have to do repeatedly.

NOTES

....

....

....

....

Group Session 5

This week's lesson discusses that Jesus is the Lamb of God who defeats all sin. Explain that seeking forgiveness for our sins is the launching point for our relationship with God. Jesus teaches that we are to remain or "abide in Him" to bear fruit. Spend time discussing what it means to abide in Jesus. Ask group members if they are as close to Jesus as they would like to be. Encourage them to identify ways they can prioritize abiding in Jesus above everything else.

NOTES

....

....

....

....

Group Session 6

This week's study discusses what it looks like to follow Jesus. Discuss the difference between merely believing God's exists and following Him as Lord. Emphasize that Jesus encourages potential Christ-followers to count the cost. Encourage group members to inventory their own beliefs and think about whether or not they are willing to follow Jesus on His terms rather than their own. Stress that the better we know Jesus the more we trust Him. Discuss why following Jesus is worth the cost.

NOTES

....

....

....

....

....

Group Session 7

In week 7, we'll spend time studying Jesus' first miracle at a wedding in Cana. Discuss that Jesus' first miracle represents the reality that the old way had passed and a new way had come. Because of Jesus, not only is our vertical relationship with God changed, our horizontal relationship with others is changed too. Encourage group members to identify ways their horizontal relationships are impacted because of their relationship with Jesus.

NOTES

Group Session 8

In this week's teaching, we'll be looking at Jesus as He enters and cleanses the temple. What John is trying to do in this gospel account is not just show you what Jesus does; but show you who Jesus is. 1). Jesus is a prophet who challenges the spiritual consumer. 2). He is a priest who cleanses us from sin. 3). He is a king who builds a temple for God's presence. Spend time discussing who Jesus is with group members.

NOTES

Group Session 9

In week 9, we look at a text that says there are men and women who believe in Jesus, but Jesus, in turn, did not entrust Himself to them. Point out that one of the things that's unique about the Gospel of John is it never uses the word *miracle*. It always uses the word *sign*. Why? Because a sign points to something other than itself. The point isn't the sign at all. The sign is meant to point at something. The kind of belief that is not saving belief is when we believe that we can make God our errand boy to get us what we really want rather than to be our Lord and Savior. Ask group members to assess the nature of their belief.

NOTES

....

....

....

Group Session 10

In this session, we are going to look at a passage that unpacks how we've been designed to relate to Jesus Christ. Key talking points: 1). Jesus is more than a teacher; He's a Savior. 2). We must be born again of water and Spirit, not just flesh. 3). We must believe.

NOTES

....

....

....

....

....

Group Session 11

This session's focal point: One can only enter the kingdom through belief in the saving work that the Son came to do, a mission that was a consequence of the love of the Father, a love that gives and sends, fully and freely, to save and redeem. Key talking points: 1). Our radical corruption from sin requires a radical redemption from God. 2). The only appropriate response is to share what we know. 3). In the Bible, Christians are primarily armed with three things: the gospel of Jesus, their story of salvation, and the Spirit of God. 4). If you're a follower of Christ today, you have everything you need to be a faithful and effective witness for the gospel of Jesus Christ

NOTES

Group Session 12

Our final lesson can be summarized in two points. We know our place, and we know our message. Talking points: 1). When we say, "We know our place," what we're saying is God is up to something, and our job is to join God in what God is up to, happily. 2). Simply put, our message is Jesus is above all.

NOTES

In the beginning was the Word...

Many new believers are encouraged to read the Gospel of John before anything else. The first three chapters are surprisingly simple yet theologically rich, understood in a moment yet challenging for a lifetime.

Through 12 sessions, Matt Chandler explores the nuance and significance of the 112 verses in chapters 1–3. Those who've experienced Matt's teaching on other subjects know of the passion and insight he brings to each study. In the end, you will have a new appreciation for the Gospel of John and for Jesus.

- Learn the nature of Christ and how true life is found in His Name.
- Depend upon God to help us believe in the name of Jesus and become His children.
- Believe in the finished work of Jesus and experience a well of abundant grace that never runs dry.
- Know who we are and who we are not because we know who Jesus is.
- Declare Jesus is the Lamb of God that will defeat all sin.
- Follow Jesus the way His first disciples did.
- Remember the old has passed away and the new has come.
- See Jesus as a Prophet who confronts us, a Priest who cleanses us, and a King who constructs the temple of true worship.
- Examine your relationships with Jesus and ensure that you know Him personally rather than simply knowing information about Him.

ADDITIONAL RESOURCES

JOHN 1–3 LEADER KIT
Includes a *Bible Study Book*, three DVDs with 17- to 38-minute video teaching sessions, and access to digital videos.

Leader Kit
005831474 $99.99

DIGITAL CONTENT
An *eBook* and video teaching sessions are available separately at lifeway.com/johnbiblestudy